NO SUCH THING AS ORDINARY

"Honest, vulnerable, refreshing, and real. In *No Such Thing as Ordinary*, Rachel Balducci shares stories and offers timeless wisdom and truth about the ways we are all called to go deeper in our extraordinary relationship with God. In a world filled with mixed messages and distraction, this book is a healthy dose of reality, hope, and real joy."

Danielle Bean
Brand manager of CatholicMom.com

"Rachel Balducci's reminder that 'our God is a God for all seasons' is surely a balm to the soul of every woman. For nearly fifteen years, Balducci's practical advice, outlook on life, and authentic living have made me a better wife, woman, and mom. Here she offers her hard-won guidance alongside wisdom from scripture. I have no doubt that this book will be the soul sister you need to help you thrive in your season of life!"

Kathryn Whitaker
Author of *Live Big, Love Bigger*

"Women desiring to grow in their faith have looked to the woman at the well as a source of encouragement. Rachel Balducci offers a refreshing and inspiring perspective to this story. You will be brought effortlessly through a journey of encounter, trust, surrender, and mission, with many other stopovers along the way."

Allison Gingras
Creator and host of *Reconciled to You*

NO SUCH THING AS ORDINARY

UNLOCKING YOUR EXTRAORDINARY LIFE THROUGH EVERYDAY ENCOUNTERS WITH JESUS

RACHEL BALDUCCI

AVE MARIA PRESS AVE Notre Dame, Indiana

TO JOANNA,
WHO HAS BEEN MANY PLACES
AND FINDS GOD EVERYWHERE

Unless otherwise noted, scripture texts in this work are taken from the *New American Bible*, revised edition © 2010, 1991, 1986, 1970 Confraternity of Christian Doctrine, Washington, DC, and are used by permission of the copyright owner. All Rights Reserved. No part of the *New American Bible* may be reproduced in any form without permission in writing from the copyright owner.

Founded in 1865, Ave Maria Press is a ministry of the United States Province of Holy Cross.

www.avemariapress.com

Paperback: ISBN-13 978-1-64680-127-5

E-book: ISBN-13 978-1-64680-128-2

Cover image © EyeEm Premium / gettyimages.com.

Cover and text design by Brianna Dombo.

Printed and bound in the United States of America.

Library of Congress Cataloging-in-Publication Data is available.

CONTENTS

Introduction vii

1. Encounter 1

2. Thirst 15

3. Gift 29

4. Trust 37

5. Conversion 47

6. Surrender 65

7. Healing through Truth 77

8. Fulfillment 93

9. Mission 103

Additional Resources 113

Notes 115

INTRODUCTION

One week toward the end of the school year, I drove over to the small Georgia town where my sister lives to help her and her husband with their four young boys. They had a new nanny lined up to start in a few weeks but needed a little help in the meantime. I was working on this book and needed the quiet time in a hotel in the evenings to get some writing done. Working from home felt frenzied: two of my college sons were back home, their comings and goings adding to the noise created by my school-age children. If I was going to sneak away for a few days, doing it before summertime seemed like a logical choice.

I spent the first evening writing all about hopes and dreams, our deepest yearnings. Over time, I saw, the reality of life means that every moment isn't a grand adventure, not in the way we pictured it would be. Over time life begins to feel quite ordinary. We have our romanticized view of our future, and then reality sets in. It's not a bad, depressing thing. It's just the truth.

The next morning, before heading to my sister's house to spend the day with her crew, I went on a run. My hotel was right across the street from my alma mater's campus, so I ran along all its paths. Passing the journalism school where I got my master's degree, I stopped for a moment and called to mind the months and years I spent in that program. Then I headed across the street past the giant football stadium that feels like sacred ground to so many people. Finally, I ended up in the quad that housed my dorm, a gorgeous, historic brick building overlooking a massive green field where students would sit on blankets to study and hang out.

It came to me that during my time living and studying on this campus, I was at the front end of my hopes and dreams, figuring out who I was and who I wanted to be. There is so much excitement on a college campus about new possibilities and prospects, so much energy around small accomplishments (lots of classes) that are leading to something bigger (a degree and a career!). I was actively moving toward a goal in those years, and life felt wide open. I had so many hopes and dreams and aspirations, and in them, I would create something extraordinary.

Being on that campus and remembering all of my twenty-something ambitions was the perfect contrast to the joy of caring for my nephews for those few days. The two sets of emotions were not at odds with one another, but they were certainly different, and I'd experienced them both in rapid succession in my own life: within ten years of getting my master's degree, I was the mother of four of my own little boys, a mother who still harbored the hopes and dreams, goals and plans, that had carried me through school.

But life, as we all know, has a way of being real. Even when all our dreams come true, there we are, just us in the middle of it. Even when our dreams come true, we are still ourselves. I'm me, with my hopes and dreams and accomplishments but also with my insecurities and anxieties. Getting the perfect degree and marrying the perfect guy doesn't change the fundamental truth of who we are at the core. It's amazing how many of those dreams I had as a student came true. But there were still parts of me, beneath the surface and deep within, that weren't and couldn't be fixed by the externals.

And if I consider what matters most to me in my life—what feels worth my time and energy now, the things that came to be that I never even planned on—what seemed like the really big stuff back then has been great, but it does not compare to the activities and experiences that have brought me true joy and great satisfaction.

This is not a book about casting away dreams, giving up, or not trying. This isn't a book about how crushing your goals isn't worth it. I'm all about having aspirations and hopes and dreams. I support you in having those. Name them, list them out, and proceed accordingly. I think you should go for it.

In this book, however, I want to focus on truth of who we are, at the very core of our beings. The things I once thought would bring me deep, abiding happiness just didn't. They were awesome and super fun and felt really good. But there is a hole in my heart, in the heart of each person, that can only be filled by God. It's a deep-seated restlessness, a restlessness that too often gets confused with personal aspirations and a desire to succeed. It's that feeling of wanting more and knowing you were made for more, of not wanting life to pass you by. It's that desire to live an extraordinary life, to BE extraordinary. It's a hole that can only be filled when we are willing to fill ourselves with something bigger than our own personal goals and plans.

This is a book about going after your dreams—but also admitting that true happiness will only come when you seek it in the right place.

"Find your delight in the LORD, who will give you your heart's desire" (Ps 37:4). This verse perfectly captures the experience of the woman at the well when she meets Jesus there. In John 4, Jesus is waiting for this woman who comes to the well in the middle of her daily grind, her chores that can't be put off, and he offers her something she didn't even know she could have: living water.

Jesus tells her that the water she is gathering at the well won't satisfy her, that she will feel thirsty again, but that the living water he offers will quench her deepest thirst.

This is the thirst we all have, the need for something bigger than just our accomplishments and dreams. If following our dreams is how we plan to fill a God-sized hole in our hearts, we will be thirsty again. It will never be enough.

But if we seek something deeper and wider and more satisfying than even our dreams, we can drink from the well that offers what nothing else can: the living water that will truly quench our deepest thirst. The living water Jesus offered the woman was the Holy Spirit, not yet named but soon to come. And we have access to that same source of love and wisdom and deep, abiding peace. We can still name and list our dreams, we can still go after our goals and hopes and plans, but we will no longer look to those temporal achievements to bring us the great happiness we seek.

We were made for more than our dreams. We were created to aim for far more—for going after a happiness and freedom that can only come from a deep union with God. When I figured out that God offers this union to each one of us, no matter where we are in life or what path we are on, it rocked my world and totally changed my life.

ONE

ENCOUNTER

So he came to a town of Samaria called Sychar, near the plot of land that Jacob had given to his son Joseph. Jacob's well was there. Jesus, tired from his journey, sat down there at the well. It was about noon.

—John 4:5–6

I thought I could be a nun. My junior year of high school I had an encounter with Jesus that left me with a great desire to serve him more. I went with a group of friends to a conference in Steubenville, Ohio, at Franciscan University. There were throngs of teenagers worshiping and praising God and the Holy Spirit descended upon us all. I was never the same again.

I came home from that conference with a desire to really follow God, to try to personally live in a way that was pleasing to him.

And then, the summer before my senior year I spent a month serving with the Missionaries of Charity, Mother Teresa's nuns, in the remote mountains of Kentucky. That whole summer I secretly hoped the sisters would tell me I was called to be one of them.

They did not.

Several years later, after my second year of college, I spent another summer with the sisters. This time we were in Harlem, New York, and this time I really meant it—I spent time in the order's chapel begging Jesus to show me his will for my life. I loved him so much and was more than willing to give everything to serve his kingdom. It was the strangest thing—despite pouring my heart out to Jesus, despite begging him to take it all, I knew clearly my call was not to the religious life. I was mystified. Here I was, willing to give everything to God, and he didn't seem to want it.

I couldn't shake the feeling that God had his special few whom he picked for service, and the rest of us were off the hook—perhaps even unremarkable. Marriage, in my mind, would be a different kind of challenge from the life of a nun, harder in many ways (after twenty-seven years of marriage this now makes me laugh, though I'm not sure why) but less extraordinary. I wanted something extraordinary, and that didn't seem to be God's plan for my life.

Being married and having a family seemed quite normal, very ordinary. Would God really use my life as a wife and mother for anything grand? Based on the marriages I had seen in books, films, and real life, marriage was not how I would define *adventurous*. But I accepted God's answer, equal parts disappointed and relieved to not hear that call, because I realized I was in love. And I had tried.

I had gone to serve the sisters with a group of other college students from my neighborhood. Later that summer, after God had not called me to religious life despite my prayers in the chapel, Paul, another volunteer with the Missionaries of Charity, became my boyfriend. He and I dated for two years, almost all long-distance, because he had just finished law school that summer and then left to work in Mexico City, while I had college to finish. We got married a few months after my graduation.

Two years after that, we had our first child, Ethan, who was (of course) the most perfect, amazing being I had ever laid eyes on. Family life was a blessing—not what I would call a grand adventure but pretty awesome just the same.

After Ethan was born, to my great surprise, all I wanted to do was stay home and do right by that boy. Up until the day he was born, I assured my boss at the newspaper that I would be back. I lasted six weeks back in the office after returning from maternity leave before turning in my notice and heading home to care for my son.

Newborn babies have a way of taking up enough time to make it hard to notice what you're missing. I was engrossed in changing his diapers and feeding him and getting myself a quick shower with my five minutes to spare. The highlight of my day was gathering my wits about me enough to load him up in a stroller and take a walk with friends.

Twenty-one months after Ethan's birth, Paul and I had another boy, Elliott, and that threw me even further into the thick of it. Another twenty-one months later, we had another son, Charles. And twenty-one months after that—another boy, August! Wow! We were pros at this.

Some seasons you are so busy trying to survive, you really don't have time to dream of anything else. With four children under six, I felt blessed and heroic to make it through the day. I got in a nice groove with the caring and feeding of boys, and that was enough. Dreams of serving God as a nun were long gone, and other dreams were on hold in the joy and frenzy of each day.

After our fourth son in five years, we figured out how to postpone having another baby using natural family planning. I started meeting regularly with an instructor who helped me understand how to use NFP to not get pregnant. Each month Paul and I would consider whether we were ready to add another baby to the mix and used the skills we learned from NFP to say, "No, we are not ready right now."

This was very important for my mental health. Life felt really hard by now—really good but very challenging. I remember one day trying to pull out of the driveway; by the time we made it to the street, every single person in the car was crying: the baby, the toddler, the two preschoolers, and me. I was just barely making it through each good but super challenging day. It was a relief to have a baby turn one without finding out I was pregnant again a few weeks later. When our fourth son turned three and no new babies were on the way, I began to enjoy some adventures outside of just keeping my four boys alive.

For two years, I did a little volunteer work. It wasn't a lot, but it felt good to reconcile who I was now with who I used to be before this intense season. Volunteering got me thinking again about my hopes and dreams and what I might one day accomplish. One day, as I was driving down the highway in our Suburban, Elton John's "Tiny Dancer" came on the radio and brought me back, in that magical way music does. Someone else was alive under the spit-up stains and mom jeans, and it was strange to remember her. Somehow this song transported me to my years as a college student, sitting in a café reading the *New York Times* and getting ready for my next class. It reminded me of a season when I could sit still long enough to drink in the world around me and think about what I had to offer that world.

Now my days were filled with keeping small children safe, fed, and happy, tidying up our home and switching over the laundry. There was no time to drink in the world around me, just a frantic effort to keep up with it. And yet it was strange: the girl I once was, the one I remembered when I heard that song, was still there—and she was amazed by how fulfilling my current life actually was. It wasn't what I had imagined would bring me joy, and yet it did.

As Augie turned five, we decided to try for "one last baby." I wasn't ready to be done raising young kids, and I felt like someone was missing from our lives. When Henry joined our family, I thought it would be really easy, like normal life with a new little mascot.

That's not how it went. Henry was born in the exact middle of summertime in Georgia, which isn't for wimps. And by now

I had boys ages five, seven, nine, and ten. Life was nuts. I was so exhausted after I gave birth to Henry that the sight of my tired eyeballs freaked out my friend Mollie, who was due to give birth a few weeks later. She admitted to me a few years later that "What happened to her, and how can I avoid that?" was her reaction upon seeing me.

Somehow giving birth after a five-year break was not as easy as I thought it would be. There was a new baby to care for along with four older brothers who had routines and commitments and lots of places to go. It was really tough for a while, and then we adjusted and life felt more manageable.

Five boys felt like a nice number, an embarrassment of riches, really. And then, three years later, God sent us one last child—a baby girl, Isabel. What a blessing! But it was during this time that I experienced a bit of a "reset"—going from the freedom I was starting to enjoy as my oldest boys got bigger back into survival mode with two younger children. I was back to trying to make it through the day and stay sane. There would be time for adventure and fun down the road. That's not where I was right then.

We made it through, putting one foot in front of the other, trusting in God's grace and his promises, and believing that even when I felt like I was drowning I always seemed to have one tip of one nostril just barely above water.

I'll take it. It was a long season of survival, but I don't remember feeling too distraught about what I was missing out on. The outside world moved too fast for me, and I was happy, at this point of motherhood, to keep my own little world in order. That was plenty. And I was totally cool with that. Until I wasn't.

When Isabel was four, we went to see the Disney hit *Moana* for some kind of a party; I sat away from Isabel, who was with a few other little girls, and it gave me the feeling of being at the movie by myself.

Moana, as I'm sure you know, is a voyager princess who saves her people by boarding a boat, leaving their small island, and heading out into the vast unknown. She is alone on her craft (with the requisite Disney animal sidekicks) and free to explore the ocean and her heart and desire for adventure and escape. She felt trapped on her own island, restless for some unknown reason, with a vision to leave and find all the answers her people desperately needed. We discover later that her wanderlust is at the core of who she is and who her people were before they stopped leaving their small island to explore the world around them.

They were voyagers. Adventure was built into their DNA.

I sat there in the dark theater fighting back sobs. Not tiny little tears but ugly sobs that would have caused a scene. I felt jealousy and a little angry. Also, I felt trapped. Who knew a Disney princess movie could stir up such angst! While Isabel enjoyed the music and dialogue, her mother sat one row behind her having a complete breakdown. An emotional meltdown. An existential crisis.

For days afterward, I thought about this movie, wrestling with feelings that seemed to come out of nowhere. *I really do love my life*, I thought, *so why am I jealous of a cartoon character who gets to ride a boat across the ocean?*

Eventually I began to connect the dots. I loved my life, but I was also in an intense season. Even though I no longer had multiple babies in diapers, no more constant feedings like before, I had six children who had a lot of needs. One preschooler, a kindergartner, and four big boys who had homework and practice schedules and so many activities for me to keep track of. I was constantly in motion but also had very limited mobility. I wasn't free to hop into any vehicle—car, boat, or even a small raft—unless I checked it out with multiple parties. I couldn't just "go" anywhere, and the stark contrast between seeing someone living her dreams and the life I was living felt like switching the filter from vivid color to black and white.

Life can be a grind, and I was in the thick of it. I just hadn't really noticed up until that moment.

I wasn't unhappy in life. That was the crazy part. I found great fulfillment in doing things like laundry and caring for and feeding my children. These were the duties I had to take care of right now, and I was still happy with my decision after having Ethan to give up my job at the local newspaper—and my dreams of being an award-winning reporter—to stay home with my family.

But in the days after watching *Moana*, I was emotional, agitated, and confused. Before that day in the theater, I hadn't been fantasizing about running away. Don't get me wrong, I'd had fantasies of escaping. Once, years before, my friend Susie and I, both postpartum with multiple babies in close succession, had made a mostly joking plan to get an apartment together where our husbands could (occasionally) visit us. Both of us, just barely staying afloat in life, needed a break. We made it through, but it was nice to think, here and there, about running away.

That's not where I was anymore, though. Even when life felt intense, I was more or less at peace. I didn't want to escape. I was trucking along just fine.

But the movie made me realize that I felt like my life was on hold. I really loved what I had going on, but now I knew there had to be more—whatever that more might be. I entered a waiting season, though waiting for what I couldn't be sure. I continued doing the things that needed doing but in a new awareness that there was more to life than laundry and carpools. My life was on some kind of pause, and even though I was happy with "today," I was aware that I was also anxiously waiting for "tomorrow."

Each of us has a deep thirst for something more that helps us push past a willingness to be mediocre. It's a desire to do something great with our lives. The challenge is figuring out what that great thing is.

Before watching *Moana*, I had started to make peace with the idea that the "great thing" I was hoping for in my life would be happening down the road; I was learning to be at peace in the here and now. I would hear the inspiring words of Jeremiah 29:11, a promise that God has great plans for each one of his people, and assume it would need to wait until I had a little more mobility and fewer basketball games to attend. A little more money and fewer small children to chase. A little more adventure, fewer obligations.

Years before all this, when my older kids were small, I had come across an incredibly inspiring quote from St. John Paul II from his address at World Youth Day in 2000: "It is Jesus in fact that you seek when you dream of happiness; he is waiting for you when nothing else you find satisfies you; he is the beauty to which you are so attracted; it is he who provokes you with that thirst for fullness that will not let you settle for compromise; it is he who urges you to shed the masks of a false life; it is he who reads in your hearts your most genuine choices, the choices that others try to stifle."[1] It hits at the heart of this deep desire for adventure and greatness, the very core of our being that yearns for something "more"—even when we can't articulate what that is.

That restless feeling within us is placed there by Jesus, according to the Holy Father. Because of him, we are inspired by tales of adventure, of living life with reckless abandon and feeling free to be who we are and not trapped by the confines of this world, this life!

But when I first read the quote, I thought it meant that Jesus gave me a thirst for meaningful adventure. When I first read that quote, I thought about all the things I was going to do—for God!—when the season was right. I focused on all the talents God had given me, all the desires I had deep within me, and formulated a plan for using those abilities for God's glory. Traveling, for Jesus! Speaking at retreats, for Jesus! Writing books, writing a newspaper column, cohosting a talk show—all for him.

And you know what? A lot of people say you can do all that now—whatever you dream of doing, you can and should be doing that very thing right now. Regardless of what your family life looks like, you need to go after your dreams using your God-given abilities. That, they say, is where real happiness will come from: doing what your heart tells you you should and living freely. Why wait?

When I first read that quote from St. John Paul II, I planned all the meaningful adventures I would have while still focusing on family life. Family life and adventure could go together, but not at the same time. Family life was an adventure to be sure. But deep within me I knew there was more, later. Now? After crying over *Moana*? I could not deny the feeling of wanting more, now. Did I need to wait to have that? Would my longing be resolved when I went after my dreams? If I decided to wait, would that restlessness be satiated when I was finally at a place in my life where I could follow my personal dreams (the non-stay-at-home-mama dreams) to start living a life that felt a bit bigger than where I was right this minute?

But we must learn to see that longing for what it is. The deep adventure Jesus has in mind for us is so much richer than a single amazing trip, a new business, or setting out on a new career path. It's not about waiting until the children are bigger so you can go have some fun already. I'm all about having fun, but focusing only on fun sells us incredibly short.

This deep adventure is bigger than following your heart and going after your dreams and finding your "true purpose." Do you see how many times I used the word *your* in that sentence? When I put myself in the center of the universe, I'm going to have a limited view of what's possible, one that's way smaller than my reality can be. Also, I'm going to end up really bored.

But more on that later.

Let me back up a little bit, to a time when I thought I was starting to experience the "more," the "greatness," the beginning of my "real" life. It's a tale of adventure and blessings and living the life I had imagined one day I might live.

Two years before *Moana*, I was invited with other writers on a trip to El Salvador to observe the work of an international charity and the charity's impact on the people it served. It was indeed life changing. We spent the week traveling to different parts of the area surrounding Santa Ana, visiting neighborhoods crowded onto the side of hills and homes nestled deep within a forest. One day, about twenty of the volunteers and workers traveled down a mountain in the back of a truck. As we made turns down the winding, washed-out dirt road, everyone had to lean to the same side of the truck to ensure it didn't tip over. South American foliage shaded us. Off in the distance was a volcano.

It was mind-blowing. It was glorious. It was way better than regular life.

Each night, we writers would return to base camp and write about the lives we saw being changed that day because of this charitable organization, and my writing helped spread the news about the work the organization did. It allowed more people to get sponsored through the charity, which meant more lives would be changed.

And then, just like that, the trip ended and I was back at home. It was early summer; all six of my kids were home from school. I was back to the hot and muggy Georgia summer, daily swim team carpool, and cleaning the house and mountains of laundry.

One morning soon after my return, while leaning over in front of the washing machine, turning a boy's dirty basketball sock right side out, I cried out to God in complaint. *This*, I declared in my heart, *this is not the best use of my gifts.*

I thought God would be mad at my poor attitude, but I remember feeling this odd sense of his love for me in that moment. He wasn't upset with my attitude; he understood it. But those emotions made me realize that there was more to the story of my frustration with spending my time doing laundry rather than writing articles that could help change people's lives. I prayed I would understand this soon.

It wasn't too long after this that I had a life-changing encounter with my friend, our neighbor Monique. Monique had a great love for the Lord and our Catholic faith. About five feet tall and skinny as a rail, she was in her late seventies when she moved to our neighborhood in Georgia from leafy Connecticut. She loved fiercely and extravagantly and was generous with praise.

Monique was exactly who I needed in my life when I was drowning in a sea of six children, at this point a baby, a toddler, and four big boys on the go. Especially because Henry, the toddler, was wild and crazy and a bit more than I had bargained for.

Life is hard with kids. Even when you see they are a gift, even when you recognize the vocation of motherhood and family life, they can still be more than you bargained for. All those years earlier, when I had made peace with not being a nun and with joyfully becoming a wife and mother, I did not make permanent peace with abandoning myself to God's will. I could say the Prayer of Abandonment, and sometimes I even meant it. But there were still so many areas in my life I was not giving to God. There were still truths to be uncovered—and finding fulfillment in the present was a big part of that, because trusting in God's plan for your life doesn't mean it's all easy. It doesn't cancel out the hard work of being a mom. And it doesn't automatically solve all your problems either. You can love your kids and also feel like life is passing you by. You can be in awe of God's great love for you with the gift of family and still have a deep longing that wonders if this is all there is.

Monique loved Henry, and she encouraged me greatly. Every time I saw her, she would tell me how pleased God was with me and especially how much he loved Henry. I always needed to hear it.

Then, one day, she handed me a piece of paper, and it started some kind of change in me—a very slight shift in my thinking that would put me on the course toward figuring some important things out.

What Monique gave me was an essay written by a woman named Catherine Doherty, the cofounder of Madonna House in Canada. For years, Monique and her husband had gone to Canada to volunteer each summer. The essay Monique shared with me, titled "The Duty of the Moment," was all about finding deep purpose and meaning in the thing I was doing in this moment. More than that, it was about believing that the thing I was doing right now—today, right here!—was the thing God was using to draw me closer to him.

> The duty of the moment is what you should be doing at any given time, in whatever place God has put you. You may not have Christ in a homeless person at your door, but you may have a little child. If you have a child, your duty of the moment may be to change a dirty diaper. So you do it. But you don't just change that diaper, you change it to the best of your ability, with great love for both God and that child. . . . There are all kinds of good Catholic things you can do, but whatever they are, you have to realize that there is always the duty of the moment to be done. And it must be done, because the duty of the moment is the duty of God.[2]

The duty of the moment was the duty of God. The thing I was doing right this minute was exactly what God was asking me to do. It was what God wanted me to be doing. It was where God was meeting me.

He wasn't drawing me out away from the reality of my life. He was meeting me right in the midst of it. Real happiness and satisfaction didn't need to be on hold for more exciting times. I could find real purpose right now, in what my current life needed from me.

In the Gospel of John, we read about the woman at the well. She goes to the well in the midday heat because the duties of her life bring her there: she is fetching water for her family. She is doing her duty—and there is Jesus, waiting for her. He knows she is coming, knows who she is and what her duties are. He sits and waits for her.

The woman meets Jesus not in spite of her daily duties but because of them. Her responsibilities bring her to Jesus. This is exciting and transformative, for the Samaritan woman and for you and me. When Jesus is sitting there waiting, everything is about to change.

Jesus's encounter with the Samaritan woman at the well in John 4 is his longest conversation with a woman in scripture. It's significant that he is there before she arrives. He meets her where her life's journey brings her—who she is, as she is, and where she is. He will do the same for us.

My view of reality, my world, and the tasks of my daily life were subtly shifting. Watching *Moana* had helped me identify a desire for adventure and fulfillment right now. Catherine Doherty helped me realize what I was doing could be an adventure if I did it for God. I had a thirst for something more, something grand, while still finding joy in the everyday stuff of doing laundry and caring for my children. But how were the two connected—this yearning for more and this satisfaction with now? *There's no way*, I thought, *that regular daily life is the grand adventure I'm yearning for.*

And it wasn't. It's not. The grand adventure is much better. I was starting to see, but it was going to take me a little more time to figure this out.

TWO

THIRST

A woman of Samaria came to draw water. Jesus
said to her, "Give me a drink." His disciples had
gone into the town to buy food. The Samaritan
woman said to him, "How can you, a Jew, ask me,
a Samaritan woman, for a drink?" (For Jews use
nothing in common with Samaritans.)
—John 4:7–9

The woman comes to the well in the middle of the day. She's
doing her daily chores, drawing water to quench her thirst. There
she meets Jesus. He asks her for something—he too thirsts. "Give
me a drink," he says. She is amazed that he would want anything
from her. She isn't worthy. She is a Samaritan woman; Jesus is a
Jewish man. For religious reasons, these are not people who run
in the same circles or even interact with each other. But Jesus
wants something from the woman—and he is about to change
her life.

He asks her for a drink; he is thirsty from his travels, and his
human, physical body needs water. But he asks her for a drink
because his real desire is for her salvation, her willingness to
accept what he is about to offer. According to a homily of St.
Augustine on the Gospel of John, "Although Jesus asked for a
drink, his real thirst was for this woman's faith."[1]

Jesus asks for water because he is thirsty. He thirsts for us.
He thirsts for me.

The woman comes to Jacob's well alone and in the heat of the day. The past weighs heavily, and she imagines her future will be more of the same. Drawing water is drudgery until she meets Jesus.

The woman at the well is thirsty, in search of something more than what her past and present circumstances are offering her. She has a past filled with mistakes. Her current situation is bleak and challenging. She is a sinner whose life is not wild with freedom and excitement. She has been married five times and is currently living with a man who is not her husband (see John 4:17–19). Her life needs change; she needs more.

Thirst—the need for water—is what brings the woman to Jesus. This is the Jesus meeting us where we are with what we need in this moment. What happens next unfolds in the choices we make about what Jesus is offering us. But in this moment, it's about our thirst, our needs, and our desire for more.

My faith journey has always felt pretty basic, perhaps even dull. Trying to call it a "conversion story" doesn't even sound right. I was raised in a Catholic home by born-again hippies who (re-) discovered Jesus when I was six months old, got me baptized, and joined a prayer group. Four years later, they moved the family across the state of Georgia to join an intentional community of charismatic Christians who were part of the Charismatic Renewal taking place in the Church in the early seventies.

I grew up knowing God loved me and understanding that I was created to know, love, and serve God and to be with him in this world and the next. These are wonderful truths, and I learned them within a vibrant group of people who had a common vision of seeking personal holiness through accountability and encouragement. Basically, an intentional Christian community is like a prayer group on steroids—it's not that the members consider themselves holier than other Christians; they just see each other so often that they can't hide from their issues with others or with themselves.

When I first read the Acts of the Apostles on my own, probably as a teenager, I absolutely recognized my life in those pages. Acts is about Christians joining together to encourage each other in holiness, to live out the gospels as authentically as possible. In order to start our community, the early members sold all their possessions and put all their money in common. They used their shared resources to buy a block of homes so members could live in close proximity. I knew people (including my parents) who spoke in tongues after being baptized in the Spirit.

Acts of the Apostles seemed pretty ordinary to me. I had no idea that this life, *my* life, was different. Or weird. But then I graduated from the private school our community established for its kids and went to college, where I soon realized that everything I assumed was common about my life was actually quite extraordinary. And weird.

And I wrestled with it. I wasn't the prodigal son—I was never actively angry about my upbringing, and for the most part, I thought its radicality was pretty awesome. But you better believe I didn't advertise it. I might tell people that I went to private school but not that every single person in my neighborhood knew each other and was actively involved in calling each other on in Christian growth.

The effect on me of being surrounded by a bunch of really wonderful people working hard to be holy was that I often felt pretty flawed. I struggled to shake the feeling that I would never be good enough, and often suffered with scrupulosity. I also came out of childhood with rejection as the filter through which I saw life. Feeling rejected was my go-to emotion.

I started to recognize this trend in college, but I didn't learn to name it until my *Moana* restlessness set in. The feelings stirred up within me demanded some form of relief. Was this the time when a person might "run"—make a significant life shift because things felt messy internally? I had no ability to change my scenery, to pick up and get distracted. I had to start dealing with these feelings, which had been there for a while but were starting to affect me in new, challenging ways.

So yes, things were complicated. From my childhood, I knew God loved me, and I knew I had a purpose in this life. But the reality of my day-to-day existence was clearly not being impacted by God's deep thirst for me. I was operating at a spiritual level that was only a little bit better than superficial.

I knew I was thirsting for something, but I didn't realize it was for more Jesus. I figured he had given me all he had to give, and I needed to find other ways to fix the insecurities and wounds that afflicted me. I assumed my yearning could only be fulfilled by circumstances outside of my ordinary life.

It's strange to reflect on this part of me because I have so many memories that don't involve this sadness. I was a very happy child, as happy as you can be in middle school (eek!), working through stuff in high school, and loving life in college. To be honest, the feelings of rejection and of not being good enough were such a part of the deal that I don't look back and feel like they ruled me. For the most part, they were small and inconspicuous, but there were plenty of them. Things were pretty calm in my school and college years, probably because I had learned to live with a certain set of truths about myself, good or bad.

Marrying right after college and heading to graduate school directly after that were experiences of God's grace and provision, of putting one foot in front of the other in a decision-making process and watching in amazement that God paved the way. We made it through living separate during the week for a period, and in between starting my coursework and defending my thesis three years later, I got pregnant and gave birth to our oldest son. I absolutely love the picture of my hooding ceremony: my supportive husband, Paul, standing next to me and my nine-month-old, Ethan, in my arms.

I would call my years of college and graduate school a season of maintenance with Jesus. I saw God's hand in orchestrating the details, but I didn't work too hard to keep him in the center of all my plans. I didn't make a huge deal of my relationship with him to my classmates, but I also didn't sever my ties. It's really easy in those busy, growing seasons to do two things: (1) to forget about God in the everyday because you are so busy planning for the future and figuring out what you want to do with yourself and (2) to forget about all your wounds and baggage because the energy and excitement you find from new adventure are a nice anesthesia for the crap you normally carry around. I was with new people, not the same friends I grew up with. And while that crew was still a part of my regular life, I didn't have to face too much music about painful memories. I didn't have to think about who I used to be as a young girl and teenager, seasons of real joy and great happiness but also of figuring out who you are (which can feel bumpy). Life was all about moving forward at a nice, fun pace. I didn't attend to old wounds because I was too busy deciding who I wanted to become.

After I finished graduate school, I framed both my diplomas, hung them on the wall, and proceeded to forget I had ever pursued higher learning. Every so often, I would notice them and appreciate the nice job I had done picking out the mat and frame. That was it. I had moved into that first, intensely absorbing wave of babies.

There wasn't a lot of time for introspection in those years, for noticing or dealing with issues like feelings of rejection, fear, and insecurity. That was God's grace—who needs to walk around acutely aware of your interior flaws when being a wife and mother is challenging enough? Also, any false sense of superiority as a mother was burned out of me after I gave birth to four boys in a row. You really get very little time on your pedestal before one of those boys runs by (very likely without a shirt on) and pushes that pedestal over.

God is always with us, working on us, but he prunes us differently in different seasons. Pruning in those years came mostly in the area of humility. God was keeping me humble, and he also gave me a good sense of humor. I really needed it then, and it continues to serve me to this day, as little boys close in age grow up to become college dudes close in age. I did see God in my life in those years, but in different, survival-skill kinds of ways.

Life circumstances can catch up to us. And when they do, we start questioning all our life choices. All the forward motion—high school graduation, career choices, university, decisions about a lifelong partner, children!—begins to slow down a bit. Even if the crazy-fast pace of having babies or traveling for work doesn't slow, some of the personal adventure does.

I realize now, looking back, that this was when my deep spiritual dehydration began. It started in those difficult years of taking four little boys to Mass, which was not exactly a pleasant experience. I even tried doing daily Mass with them a few times, and it generally resulted in tears. For me. I would not say things were bad for me spiritually, but I wouldn't realize until that moment watching *Moana* that I wanted something more. Life felt ordinary. I wanted extraordinary.

I began to sense things deep within me that needed fixing. I wanted "more," though I wasn't quite sure what that meant or how to get it. I was thirsty.

I was becoming more aware of my two conflicting inner landscapes—that I was known and loved by God and also that I experienced deep feelings of insecurity and rejection and a fear I would never be enough. The first was a set of truths, and the second was a set of lies.

And I was getting tired of the truths being drowned out by the lies.

The thing about lies, though, is they are very hard to dismiss. I am a big believer in spiritual warfare and in Satan being the great accuser. But I am so slow to catch on to the lies I believe. My soul was thirsting for more of the Lord, but I had to come to believe I was worthy enough to receive God's love.

Before I go further, I want to share a story with you. When I was working through these emotions years ago, I was a blogger who blogged all the things on a daily basis. I remember writing my way through one of these emotional introspection roller-coasters one night and a commenter basically saying, "Jesus died for you, so just get over yourself and accept it." Like it was prideful of me not to just receive God's love already.

If you feel that way right now, then God bless you. I'm happy that you are able to put mind over matter and just do what you know is right. That's pure grace right there, and praise God for it! Getting to a place of leaning into God's great love for me—of learning to receive it and operate out of it—it's been life-changing. But it didn't happen overnight for me.

Here's the really awesome part for those of us who thirst for the Lord and can't quite just accept it all. It blows my mind: Jesus thirsts even more for you.

As parched and weary and wanting as my soul is, Jesus has an even deeper desire for me. He waits at the well, and he offers me water that will leave me deeply satiated in every area of my life.

Times in life of great thirst and struggle often start us thinking that something other than what we are doing right now is the thing that will bring true happiness. You start to look ahead, to when you will be able to make a home together with the love of your life, to when small humans are more mobile or can be left alone, or to that blessed season when you can have two minutes in a row of uninterrupted thought. For years, I assumed I would be truly happy when we finally replaced the blue laminate countertops in the kitchen with granite.

The thing that will really solve all my problems, we begin to think, *is something outside of this time and space. If only I could follow my dreams, then I would be truly satisfied.*

We thirst to get to the place where we find our true worth and identity. We want to know who we are, and what that means personally. Our feeble human minds think that these things come from what we do, that who we are is defined by our latest accomplishment. And when you spend your days changing diapers, cleaning lab equipment, or filling out insurance forms, that may feel like a crummy thing to be defined by. We don't feel like we're living any dream, let alone *the* dream.

Recognizing my real thirst came when I had absolutely nothing to offer anyone—my husband, myself, society, or the world around me—except my ability to make it through the day. It's not glamorous to admit that; it's what I would call my "rock bottom" season. I had survived the first wave of a pack of boys by leaning into that season of making it through the day. Then I got mobility, started doing things outside the home, and started enjoying an identity outside of just wiping the next runny nose and making it to the next nap time. By the time our fourth son turned five, I was active outside the family sphere. I did as much school stuff with my boys as I could. I was happily blogging every day, did freelance work for a local parish, and was the columnist for our diocesan paper. So much fun!

And then our openness to life yielded two more Balducci babies.

And that was the end of mobility. It was even harder than before because this time I had a life outside of the baby and toddler—a few side projects and also big boys to manage. I was barely making all that work. In order to survive the next few years, I knew I had to pull back to a bare-bones existence. Paul told me I could go to as many sporting events as I wanted, but I was also free to stay home with the littles (as we still call them!) in order to survive.

No more carpools; no more field trip chaperoning. No more room mom responsibilities; no more being the person who stepped in and got the job done. In order for my brain to stay moderately free of anxiety and dread, I had to assess my top proprieties (husband, kids, and household management) and step back from everything else.

Here is the absolutely most crazy part of my story: it was in this season that God really showed up. Jesus was sitting at the well waiting for me. In my daily chores, in my everyday existence, he appeared and said, "I've got something more for you. Are you ready?"

It all started with a drive around the block.

I only had baby Isabel with me that morning. The big boys were all in school by this point, and Henry was in preschool. After dropping Henry off at preschool, I had this overwhelming urge to go to adoration. I could sneak in there for about fifteen minutes if Isabel stayed asleep and just soak up Jesus's presence.

Except I couldn't find a parking space. Something was going on at the Catholic school adjacent to the adoration chapel, and there was no parking anywhere. There was a free space for the senior center next door, but I couldn't steal that. My only option was to park several blocks away and lug Isabel in her car seat. That was a deal breaker.

I went away sad.

And yet despite the fact that I couldn't attend adoration, something deeper was happening: a tiny breakthrough in my relationship with Jesus, a more profound recognition of my need for God. My soul was thirsting for the Lord, and I went away sad when I could not be with him. Instead of feeling relieved to be off the hook for this inconvenience, I knew spending time with Jesus was exactly what I desired.

In the months surrounding this failed attempt at adoration, something else was happening—a stirring deep inside me, a restlessness for something more.

But I was not in a position to let that *more* that I desired be anything too earth-shattering, from a worldly view. My restlessness could not be cured by a trip because I was too busy to travel. My thirst could not be slaked by a new project because I had no energy to start something new. No new book to write, no project to begin, no place to go to escape this angst. These feelings creeping in were the same as so many before me had experienced and so many more will experience on their own journey toward personal freedom. This restlessness we feel deep inside of us cannot be stilled by a quick fix or a distraction. Our souls thirst for Jesus, and he waits to quench that thirst.

What made this moment different for me, what changed everything, was that because of my life circumstances, I wasn't able to get confused about what my restless feelings meant. I knew they did not mean that my life was a sham or my marriage was busted. They didn't signal a need to start a new career or move to a new town.

Change and adventure can be great, but the ability to recognize where the desire for these things comes from is crucial. For me, these inner stirrings could have meant any number of things, and when I discovered that they signaled a thirst for something deep and abiding, I was so relieved and grateful that I held out for something that would satisfy that thirst rather than something superficial to distract me from it.

I found myself really hungering to spend time with Jesus despite the busyness of my life. That's how I knew this restlessness wasn't about me—on my own power, I would have opted for something totally different, like a kid-free vacation. As evidenced by my drive around the block praying for a parking space at the adoration chapel, I was hungry in a new way.

What was holding me back from exploring this more? What was keeping me from jumping in to a deeper relationship with Jesus? Well, for one thing, I needed proof. Were these feelings really God pulling me closer to himself? And why me? How in the world was I on his radar? Of all the people God might be reaching out to, why a stay-at-home, barely-not-drowning wife and mother?

After Paul and I got married, we went to a football game at my alma mater's huge, packed stadium with his sister and her family (I had never gone to a game as a student—sad but true). It was quite a day. Even though I have five sons and five brothers, I'm not what you would call a sports fanatic. I love cheering for teams, but I'm just as happy to enjoy fellowship with the other bleacher moms as I am to get hyped for the game. On this day in the massive arena, my attention was less on the game and more on the fans. So many fans! In a sea of football lovers, I was but one tiny speck. A grain of sand on the dense shores, a drop of water in a very large bucket.

How in the world, I marveled, *could God possibly have me on his radar? It doesn't make sense!*

In those days, I wasn't actively engaged in conversation with God so much as thinking about him. I didn't ask him to prove his love. I just marveled at how he could possibly keep up with it all and even doubted that he did. I had never before been in a space with so many people, and I was painfully aware of them all. *There are a lot of people,* I thought, *There's no way I'm special.*

Like the woman at the well, I was thirsty, both at that football game and in the time following my failed visit to adoration. Like the woman at the well, I met Jesus in my daily life. As he did for the woman at the well, Jesus was waiting for me, offering something far better than I could ever have imagined: himself. Like the woman at the well, I could not believe I was worthy to take him up on his offer.

I was unworthy and unsure, tired with nothing to give. But God was responding to something deep within me crying out. He was gently guiding me to the solution to my restlessness. God was going to help me get where I needed to be.

We got a new priest at our parish in these months. Fr. Brett's style of holiness felt revolutionary. He had this way of inviting Jesus into every aspect of his life, and while it surely took a lot of energy, it seemed to come quite naturally. Fr. Brett wanted to be a saint; I didn't doubt this for a minute.

I started meeting with Fr. Brett every few months, and without realizing it, he became my unofficial spiritual director. We delved into the internal angst that I couldn't shake and that I was tired of carrying around. I was so over feeling agitated with certain people in my world, but I felt helpless to shake feelings of jealously and pettiness and extreme judgmentalism. This had started creeping in when Isabel was a baby. For years I was so happy and busy with school adventures and wedded bliss and new babies that it wasn't a struggle. At some point, though, this negativity crept in and became a real problem for me. It was debilitating, though I didn't realize how bad it was at the time.

Those first meetings were life changing because they shifted the focus of my struggles away from the sins of those around me and toward my own woundedness. Spiritual direction helped me begin the painful and revolutionary journey of recognizing what inside of me needed healing. God didn't want me to live this way, and he was giving me the tools to change.

Around this time, I had a conversation with a trusted friend, Dan, who is a little older than me. He had shared years before about a journey of contemplative prayer God had taken him on. Both God and Dan had been thirsting. Dan referred to this as "deeper conversion." As he described it, God was drawing Dan closer to himself, and Dan was holding on for the ride. And what a ride it was! Because he was willing to open up, let God in, and sit in silence, Dan felt his life being transformed. All his areas of need and want, of wounds and hurts and insecurities, were being healed.

When he had shared this story, it had felt very far ahead of where I was but also resonated with me. I knew the current stirring in my soul had to be a God thing, but where to go from here? I decided to ask Dan what he thought.

He directed me to *The Cloud of Unknowing*, a book about contemplative prayer—sitting in silence and asking God to show up. This book was revolutionary for me because for so long I equated prayer with sitting somewhere, feeling restless, and telling God all the things I wanted him to fix. Up to this point, prayer had been something I always meant to do and didn't manage to do enough of, which made me feel guilty.

Unfortunately, when prayer is about just telling God what's going poorly in your life, what needs fixing, then time in prayer can be a little nerve-wracking. When you're carving out twenty precious minutes of your precious day to think all about everything that's going wrong in your world, of course it's anxiety-inducing!

If this was what prayer was all about, no thank you!

But once again, my soul knew more than my head and my heart. My soul was hungry—thirsty!—and yearning for way more than this kind of relationship with God. I decided to try this new approach: show up, sit in silence, and see what happened.

I won't lie, it made my head hurt. For the first four or five weeks, my brain felt sore after my contemplative prayer time. It felt like very heavy lifting to lift nothing. Sitting and not fixating was so counter to my overactive imagination and control-oriented personality that I wasn't quite sure how to proceed. But I kept showing up. I wanted more, and I wasn't going to give up easily.

"Holiness will solve all your problems," Fr. Brett declared one day at Mass. He also liked to tell us that love inspires more than the Law requires. Both of these concepts blew my mind. I wanted a piece of this kind of holiness. I wanted a holiness that was so all-encompassing that it would solve all my problems. The idea of love inspiring me to do more than what the Law told me to do—now that sounded like real freedom. It sounded way better than my current petty way of feeling quite proud of myself for being nice to the prickly pears in carpool line. I didn't want to live this way; it felt like carrying around a duffel bag of bricks. But of my own accord, I was helpless to change.

I was anxious. And insecure. And mean. A sinner who experienced rejection. I knew God loved me, but somehow I was not seeing the connection between my restless feelings, the contemplative prayer I was trying, and the love I was trying to embrace that would ask more of me than the Law required.

I was thirsty for a change. Something had to give.

My heart and soul were in a stirred-up state of wanting more but also not being able to just pack up and follow my dreams. The restlessness could not be solved by going on a three-month mission trip or selling everything to start new. Whatever I had going on was way bigger than finding myself in a foreign country or "washing my face" or "leaning in" to what I felt like doing in that moment. I couldn't walk away and completely start over, but something inside me wanted to feel an equally revolutionary change.

And then one day, a friend called—a boy I grew up with who had had a fabulous conversion experience and was now a friar. He called so I could conduct an interview with him for a newspaper article, the tiniest bit of freelance work I was creeping back into doing. When he shared his story, I started heaving deep, uncontrollable sobs. I could barely breathe. I could barely talk.

Something was about to break wide open.

THREE

GIFT

Jesus answered and said to her, "If you knew the gift of God and who is saying to you, 'Give me a drink,' you would have asked him and he would have given you living water." [The woman] said to him, "Sir, you do not even have a bucket and the well is deep; where then can you get this living water?"

—John 4:10–11

The woman is at the well, doing her daily chore. Jesus is there waiting for her and offers her water that will quench her deepest thirst. But Jesus doesn't have a bucket—she's confused. What could Jesus possibly be offering? And how will it really quench her thirst?

The woman thinks that the only thing that will quench her thirst is water from the well. Her understanding is that the feeling of thirst that she has is for water. She understands this feeling and has learned from life experience that using her bucket to scoop out water for her to drink will quench that thirst. And yet she is thirsty again and again and again. She must come back to the well every day because she will always need more water.

Jesus tells her that what he offers is something that will truly quench her thirst—she will no longer need to seek for the thing that will truly satisfy her. She will have found it.

Of course, when the woman showed up at the well that day, she was really just coming for plain water. She didn't expect a life-changing encounter with anyone. She was doing her duties, marking that item off the list. But she also had burdens she carried with her. When he offered her the deeper waters, Jesus knew about her past mistakes, and he loved her still.

When Br. Malachy called me from the friary in New York, I wasn't expecting our call to go the way it did. I was interviewing him from down in Georgia, in the same neighborhood where he grew up, for our diocesan newspaper, to tell the story of his decision to join the Franciscan Friars of the Renewal. His story is inspiring, but I had heard it before.

Larry, as he was known before becoming a friar, had grown up in a Catholic family with parents who loved Jesus. In middle and high school, he got in trouble at school. Sometime after graduating, he started following rock bands, living out of a van and driving from show to show. It was supposed to be a fun time, but for Larry, it was not.

One night, at an epic show, Larry saw the emptiness of his life. Looking around the concert, he had a moment of clarity and saw that the sex and drugs and music were all fleeting. God gave him a moment of grace where he saw the laughter and dancing and knew it would be gone in the morning. The fun of this moment, he realized, was not true joy. He felt deep within himself that there was more to life than the constant highs and lows of partying and crashing, chasing one experience after another in hopes of being fulfilled. Larry even knew what that more was—and would be able to admit, not long after, that God had been gently keeping himself on his radar. After his conversion, Larry admitted that he always felt God was calling him to more. Larry hadn't forgotten about God, but he had been happy to ignore him for a while.

Not long after that concert experience, Larry was back in our neighborhood, where a missionary priest was staying with friends. The priest offered Larry the chance to go to confession, and that confession changed everything for him.

After Larry had told all of his sins, the priest looked at Larry with a giant smile and said, "I always knew you had a good heart." That was it. That one sentence melted Larry. He saw God's love. What he experienced in that comment and in that absolution was a taste of the depths of God's healing and forgiveness—but it was more than that.

This was the point in Br. Malachy's story when I realized that the whole amazing "dude at a rock show returns home because he has a moment of truth" summary wasn't the story at all. It was merely a nice little prologue. The real story was the absolute freedom and joy that oozed out of Br. Malachy now that he had tasted the living water, the *more* that he had once searched for in the roadie lifestyle and had instead found in God. Though we were on the phone, I could hear in his voice that he could not stop smiling.

I had come into the interview jaded, assuming Br. Malachy would tell me things I already knew. We grew up in the same neighborhood and went to the same school. Our parents were part of this same Christian community. I didn't have a really amazing conversion story like Br. Malachy, but I figured we had both arrived at a similar point—we were people working to say yes to Jesus—so I wouldn't learn anything from this interview.

But by the end of our conversation, I knew there was so much more that God wanted to offer me. He was sitting at the well, waiting to meet me exactly where I was and take me somewhere unknown and life changing.

The irony is that this moment of realization about God's deep, personal plan for me came when I was speaking to someone who had left his former life to join something radical. I wasn't in a position to do that. But what I was able to hear from Br. Malachy was about leaving your spiritual place.

Jesus sat waiting. He held out his hand and offered me, Rachel, wife and mother of six, the same freedom and adventure and transformation that he offered Br. Malachy. As I cried and listened to Br. Malachy speak, I knew my options in responding were exactly the same as his: yes or no.

What would it be?

Jesus sits and waits, wanting to offer us more. But unless we are willing to quiet ourselves to listen to him, we can easily misunderstand this offer. In our human brains and understanding, we see gifts from God the way the world sees them. We might focus on worldly success and achievements or think that when God offers to give us goodness, it means we will live a life without suffering or pain.

"Peace I leave with you; my peace I give you," Jesus says in John 14:27. "Not as the world gives do I give it to you. Do not let your hearts be troubled or afraid." Here is the heart of the gift Jesus is offering, and his promise that it will quench our deepest thirst. If we are content to remain at a surface-level relationship with Jesus, where we merely list our problems and ask him to solve them, we sell Jesus really short. We are left needing our bucket filled again and again because we aren't taking advantage of the real, thirst-quenching water.

The rumblings of this realization that I had been content with merely telling Jesus my problems but not accepting the life-giving water he offers began the day I talked with Br. Malachy. It wasn't what he said. It was the hope of his story—the joyful expectation I experienced in hearing from someone who had been in the dark and was now in the light, in the very center of a very bright light.

My friend had been deeply thirsty and had recognized his need for a deep encounter with Jesus in the most unexpected place—a smoke-filled rock concert! This man who was tired of trying to quench his thirst with what the world had to offer had met Jesus in his daily routine and dared to respond, "OK. I'll give this totally new thing a try."

His story is not simply about leaving his life and becoming a friar; that decision was a few years in the making. The heart of his story is his willingness to listen to Jesus's offer of something more, say yes, and be transformed to his core.

This is what I heard. This is what I wanted.

What does this gift, this transformation, look like? "They will know we are Christians by our love," I remember singing growing up. Even as a little girl, I knew that such love could only come from Jesus. But as life continued, the practical work of following Jesus became more about checking things off a list—making it to Mass, saying the Rosary, spending time in prayer. Somehow that special love got lost in the practical duties of following Jesus.

Real relationship with Jesus meant being willing to go deeper and see where he would take me. That was my takeaway from my conversation with Br. Malachy. That was the heart of what made me heave guttural sobs while trying to express my excitement about what I felt God might want to do with me. God was so much bigger and wider and vaster than my human brain could comprehend, and I was tired of trying to put all of that power in a box that worked for me. By limiting my relationship with Jesus to a list of things I needed fixed, by seeing Jesus as way high in the sky and not down here with me in the moment—I was keeping him out of depths of who I was. Who I am. And God was offering me something big—power? love? freedom? I just had to stop trying to stifle it in my life.

Was I brave enough to take him up on his offer?

Here's where I was at in life around this time: very tired. Tired of feeling like being kind was a chore. Tired of carrying my emotional baggage, past wounds, and agitation at the world around me. Tired of feeling like being nice to people I didn't really like was some heroic deed. Tired of having so many people I didn't like. Tired of being petty and judgmental and persnickety.

I had put God and his power in a box and was exhausted from trying to be a good Christian on my own steam. But God stirred something in me during that conversation with Br. Malachy, filling me with hope and excitement. God was on the move, and I was getting brave enough to say, "Here I am, Lord! I will go, Lord."

Those words come from "Here I Am, Lord," a song by John Michael Talbot that made a big impression on me at sixteen, when I went with a group of students from our small Christian school to a summer conference in Steubenville, Ohio—a big retreat put on by Franciscan University. It was the first time I was around charismatic worship outside of our community. I couldn't believe my eyes—there were so many young people willing to sing and pray and worship like this. It was so encouraging.

"Here I Am, Lord" focuses on going where Jesus needs us to be, and I was so moved by the lyrics that I couldn't help but raise my arms in praise. I wanted to be sent by Jesus, to go where he led me. As a junior in high school, I wasn't sure what it meant to be the hands and feet of Jesus, but I suspected it meant going to Africa. That just seemed right: serving the Lord and doing what he asked me to do would surely involve going somewhere far away and learning a new language. I was up for it.

All these years later, as a mama working on a newspaper article from home, I felt a new meaning to that song stirring inside me. I had offered myself to Jesus years ago in my willingness to have a religious vocation but didn't hear the call. I got my degrees, started a job, got married, had babies, and found my life on an autopilot that didn't seem to involve anything too radical for Jesus.

And now this conversation with a monk, an excitement about what God could do, and a reminder of a song about going where God was leading me. I began to realize that God was leading me not further out but further in.

Following him, I was heading into deeper waters.

I grew up going to the ocean, living less than three hours from the coast here in Georgia. And I'll tell you, I found the waves scary after twice being slammed into the sand by a wave I never saw coming, first as a little girl and later as a teenager.

Paul and I have been vacationing at the beach with our family since Augie was six weeks old. As our kids grew older and taller, we started all being able to hang together in the deeper waters. Because there was no scary drop-off at the beach we visited, we could enjoy bobbing up and down in the waves and take advantage of the thrilling big waves without being swept out to sea.

Except I was still getting slammed down by the waves. It was frustrating, and I was tired of just hanging out in the shallow water. I didn't understand how the rest of my family could enjoy the giant waves that barreled toward us without feeling complete terror.

"What am I doing wrong?" I finally asked my husband and kids one day. And around that time I noticed it—every time a giant wave started to crash over our heads, they would simply duck under the water.

Just like that.

There was no trying to steady themselves as the giant wave crashed atop their heads. There was no trying to jump high enough to avoid being swept up by it. They simply ducked, the wave crashed, and they were completely unscathed because they *went deeper*.

From then on, every time a giant wave began to form off in the distance, instead of trying to swim to shore to avoid it, push myself high enough to get over it, or steady myself to withstand it, I simply dove under it. I went deeper, and the wave could no longer harm me.

This revelation, this going deeper, was exactly what Jesus was offering in his living water. It involved a whole new way of operating. Drinking the water that Jesus offered meant not getting caught up in the swells of the world. It meant living at a level of relationship with Jesus that was about more than telling him the latest agitation, the latest thing I needed Jesus to fix.

Jesus offered to the woman at the well—to me, to us—his help in avoiding getting knocked over, dragged down, battered, and bruised by the woes of the world. He didn't promise a lack of suffering or pain, but his living water spares us much of the pain and exhaustion we suffer when we try to operate from our own power. His gift of living water is an offer of more freedom than we could ever dream of, because we aren't constantly picking ourselves up from the most recent agitation and negative interaction. Instead, his power sustains and guides us through these troubles.

Being sustained by his living water also means that when things do go badly, we seek Jesus in the midst of the trouble. We can feel his guiding hand with us and sense his presence not just in our victory but also in our suffering.

I felt a longing in my soul for something deeper and grander. It wasn't my family that I wanted to escape; it was the snares and threats of the devil. It was the pettiness of my human nature. I wanted to flee from heaviness and sadness in my heart. I wanted to let Jesus into all the parts of my heart and soul, not because I knew I was holy but because I was tired of doing things on my own strength. I couldn't spiritually jump higher than the big waves, and I was tired of getting knocked down. The idea of this deep thirst for more being quenched was very appealing, even if I didn't understand how it would work.

Jesus was offering a gift. Did I have the guts to take him up on the offer?

FOUR

TRUST

Jesus answered and said to her, "Everyone who drinks this water will be thirsty again; but whoever drinks the water I shall give will never thirst; the water I shall give will become in him a spring of water welling up to eternal life."
—John 4:13–14

Here is the moment of truth. Jesus offers the woman at the well something beyond anything she thought possible. Does she trust him? I bet this was a difficult decision for the woman. She had been married several times before, and was known to keep the company of many men. I don't think life had been very kind to her thus far. Trusting someone might have been scary.

Following Jesus is scary. He makes a lot of big promises. Do we really believe what he says? What does he promise us, anyway? Sometimes being a follower of Jesus gets a bad rap; it can sound like a list of rules and regulations instead of something so much better than that—real freedom. And what does real freedom mean?

These were the thoughts and emotions pulsing through me. Wanting to go to the adoration chapel, not just to check it off an item on a to-do list but to spend time with Jesus—that was new. I found myself unsatisfied with the status quo, but not because I wanted to be better than others: I was beginning to accept my "inner poverty," as Fr. Jacques Philippe calls it in *Searching for and Maintaining Peace*. I was starting to find God in my daily life, seeing that perhaps what I was doing right now was what God wanted me to be doing. And I had this thirst to connect more deeply with him.

These were all minor miracles, simple moments of grace that were becoming transformative. And one of it was my doing. It was an awakening, a stirring in my soul that needed to be understood.

Also, I began to experience a deep desire to be free of selfish clinging, of the many little ways I focused so much on myself. I wanted to be done with becoming agitated quickly, of needing to always get my way. I was tired of feeling rejected and having to fight feelings of inferiority and pride. I was so tired of being a negative person. Even if I managed to be nice on the outside, I lived with constant inner turmoil. Some of this is the "human condition," but the underlying theme of several books I read in this season was that God was bigger than all of my anxiety and fear and that he wanted me to be free of this distress.

Perhaps it was possible to live without these burdens. If that was true, how did I get there?

Maybe my two strong desires were connected: the desire to connect more with my Creator and the desire to love my life, the one I was living right now, to the fullest; the desire to trust Jesus and the desire to be truly happy. But I couldn't be sure, not just yet.

Of course, crying on the phone with a monk felt over the top. What the heck was going on?

God was doing something, but I wasn't quite sure what it was. It felt crazy and scary. *Is this really the direction I should be going in?* I wondered. *Is an inward focus really the right move?* For so long I'd been looking down the road to when I'd be able to "do" more—for God and for myself. Seeking and following Jesus and doing big things for God felt like an adventure that would certainly happen, I thought, but not here in my hometown or in my own home. Such quests would need to be deferred until I was more mobile, until my kids were bigger and I had the time and energy to have an outward focus. It would happen, and I had a sense of what that joyful shift would look like—me doing something that was all about others, those not in my own home and backyard.

Instead, I was being drawn inward. That felt weird. Navel gazing isn't exactly celebrated in some circles. It sounds prideful and vain, self-centered and self-indulgent—not descriptors I wanted to be associated with.

But here's the other phrase that kept coming my way: "Be who God meant you to be, and you will set the world on fire." St. Catherine of Siena said it, and boy, did I need to hear it.

You can't know who God meant you to be unless you are willing to turn inward and do some self-examination.

At this point, what I knew about myself was a false identity: too loud, too insecure, too quick to gossip, too quick to feel rejected. I knew a lot about what I didn't like about myself. Underneath all this distortion was who God made me to be, but I was clinging so tightly to my false self, to all the ways I'd messed up and caused problems and been mean and petty, that I couldn't see who God made me to be. I had to learn how to acknowledge and love that person.

But for a long time, I thought self-love was the worst form of pride because the inward focus has become terribly distorted these days. There is a move for self-awareness and self-examination, but the core of this focus is often personal feelings. We base our next move on what feels good and right, what we personally think we need.

Unfortunately, this can have disastrous results. Families get torn apart; lives get upended. We become the sum of our wanderlust and our skill set, not bothering to ask God what he would have us do. Maybe we tune God out because we're afraid he might tell us something we don't want to hear.

God did give us feelings, and feelings are not to be ignored. A few years earlier I had met with a counselor because I struggled to overcome certain mental hurdles—I would get in a negative spiral of crazy thinking that would take over my life. The counselor was very helpful, and my takeaway from that meeting was that I needed to add some basic skills to my mental health arsenal, things like perspective, changing the channel, and shifting my narrative.

Not long after that counseling session, I began meeting with a spiritual director with a little more regularity. Mostly it was when I had a "flare-up"—an agitation that I couldn't move past. With so much hurt and rejection piled up inside of me, I needed to periodically shovel things out. Eventually, I began seeing her every month, whether I had a crisis or not. The discussions we had helped put my flawed thinking under the lens of Jesus and his great love for me; they began to break down the negative cycle and break up the bondage. Also, because we were meeting regularly, I was able to explore more about my relationship with Jesus than just my troubles. I was having some victories, too!

In one meeting during this time, my spiritual director explained that feelings can help us determine if something is off in our life, but we need good counsel and personal maturity to analyze what those feelings mean and how we should act on them. For me, this realization was an important step in leaning into a trust relationship with Jesus, the heart of which is acknowledging that Jesus loves you and wants to be a part of every aspect of your life and your being. He cares about it all. Jesus wanted true healing for me, and he also loved me exactly as I was.

If this thought makes you feel smothered, that's okay. Letting God into every part of my life makes me feel smothered at times too. But it's in facing your fear of inviting Jesus into every single part of your being that trust begins.

Trust in Jesus is what breaks down the disconnect between who we dream of being and the reality of our daily existence. Trust in him connects wanting to live a life of grand adventure and also just wanting to get through the day. Jesus wants to be a part of the really excellent and also the really painful.

A few years ago, my husband and I traveled to the Holy Land to celebrate our twenty-fifth anniversary. We went with our good friend Fr. Tim, who (two weeks before leaving for seminary) had been the best man in our wedding. Tim and Paul have been the best of friends since they met when they were fourteen. They had both moved to Augusta because their parents had all heard and followed a call to live in community with other committed Christians. Paul's friendship with Fr. Tim has made me quite the beneficiary of all those yeses to Jesus.

Our pilgrimage group included the three of us, Fr. Tim's mother, and parishioners from several of the churches where Fr. Tim has served. We saw a lot in our travels that really brought to life Jesus as a man and all the biblical places we read about and hear about each week at Mass. We walked the Way of the Cross, visited the place where Elizabeth greeted Mary, and touched the rock on which the Cross was erected.

One of our most profound stops was at a place I had never thought very much about. Fr. Tim explained that we don't talk much about the site because it's where Jesus was taken after the apostles had scattered from the Garden of Gethsemane. Peter followed and entered the courtyard but could not go inside. By the next morning, they were with Jesus again. But the religious authorities who took Jesus from the garden brought him to the home of Caiaphas, the high priest, where he spent the night in a dungeon before being brought to the Romans the next morning.

It was an actual pit, the place Jesus spent the night before his crucifixion. Only a few hours earlier, he had been enjoying a meal with some of his very best friends; now he was being lowered through a narrow opening into a pit too deep to step into. The next morning Jesus would be on trial before Pontius Pilate and then scourged; then he would carry his Cross to his Crucifixion.

That pit stood out to me. As his ministry ended and before his dying began, Jesus spent those overnight hours in that pit.

We visited St. Peter in Gallicantu, the church built on top of this sacred site. Now there are stairs and a light, and yet the Sacred Pit, as it is called, is still a tight space. From down at the bottom, you can see the small opening so very high above.

One day after we got back from our trip, when I felt sad and worried about something, Jesus reminded me of that place he was lowered into. He showed me that my hurts and fears were a form of that pit; the wounds I carried and the suffering I've caused and experienced were like deep caverns in my soul—dark, deserted places where I feel totally alone.

Jesus showed me he is there with me. He wants me to allow him into all of these places so he can shine his healing light into them.

This is abandonment. It's the purest form of trust.

When we feel abandoned in those dark places, Jesus wants to be there with us. He asks that we abandon ourselves to him—that we hand these dark places over to him. It's not because he's a control freak. It's because he can offer the healing and deep peace that only comes from the Father.

Abandonment is the make or break in fulfillment. What do we seek in order to fill these deep spaces in our soul? When we feel lonely, where do we turn? When we feel overlooked, what do we strive for? When our heart feels restless, do we understand that, as St. Augustine said, it will never rest until it rests in the Lord?[1]

We are created by God in a unique and marvelous fashion. There is only one you, and what God is doing deep within you, in all those secret, sacred spaces, he cannot do in anyone else. But how do we learn to really believe that truth? How do we get to the place of being willing to open our clenched fists and release everything to Jesus?

We have to learn to trust God and to seek evidence of his goodness. When we examine our feelings and emotions, we have to take that first scary step of saying, "I believe in your love for me, Jesus. Prove it." God can handle those kinds of requests, perhaps even when we are a little bossy about it. Sometimes, when I'm feeling bold, I'll say something to the Lord like "Jesus, I love you! Knock my socks off today!"

But when I make those kinds of requests, I then have to be willing to find Jesus in my day. When I am feeling sad, where do I find Jesus? When I am happy, where is Jesus? As I move throughout my day, as I make decisions and interact with others, am I aware of God and his guiding hand, or do I act and think as though it's all about me and my desires?

Trust is about letting someone else lead the way. That's a really scary thing to do. And we can only really lean into that kind of trust relationship when we give God the chance to prove his goodness to us. If we want God to prove it, we have to get in the habit of looking for that proof.

When I first started traveling as a speaker and an author, I was terrified to fly. I'm not ashamed to admit it. I would get sick to my stomach when it was time to book my flight. I worried about crashing and getting claustrophobia, about being in a middle seat or too far back. I knew nothing about how airplanes worked and actually suspected that it was my anxiety that was keeping us all safe in the air. *If I stay alert and aware of all that can go wrong, then nothing bad will happen,* was my stellar reasoning process.

As I started to fly more often and grew tired of being terrified, I began to do a little research. One day I walked next door and asked our neighbor, a retired military pilot, how in the world it could possibly be safe to fly. He patiently explained to me the basics of how an airplane worked, how it stayed in the air, and how the atmosphere was its own form of matter (like water!). After that, I felt a little safer.

And then I flew. And arrived safely.

And I flew again. And arrived safely.

The more this kept happening, even when there were bumps in the flight or I got a bad seat or we got stuck on the tarmac longer than I would prefer, the more proof I had of the goodness of airline travel. I finally reached a point where I unclenched all the tightly wound body parts that I thought were keeping me safe and began to trust the pilot and the plane. It was a very liberating experience.

It's understandable to ask God to prove things to us. We are called to trust, but that's not an easy endeavor. We need evidence of God's trustworthiness in order to move forward in that relationship.

And we have to be willing to let go.

If you've ever had an extended season caring for a sick loved one, you understand how challenging control can be. It's actually more exhausting to try to maintain your tight grip on the situation than it is to release the situation. "Jesus, I trust in you," is my mantra in these times, both because I know it to be true and because I want to believe it more every day.

This trust relationship begins when we are willing to invite Jesus into our emotions. We take the scary step of really examining how we feel and then asking God to shine his light on that area. We ask ourselves, *What parts of my life am I trying to keep Jesus out of? And why?*

"Lord, I am not worthy that you should enter under my roof, but only say the word and my soul shall be healed." These words from the Mass are what it's all about. We aren't worthy, and yet Jesus wants to be with us. He doesn't want to be left out of any of it—the good stuff, the bad stuff, the ugly and scary and unpleasant bits. He wants to be with us even if it's a scary pit.

Learning to trust means learning to believe that he wants to
be with us, but not to boss us around or tell us how bad we are
or control us. It means really believing that welcoming Jesus into
every part of our being, into our heart and soul and deep into
our core, will offer real freedom and healing, breaking off our
shackles instead of making them feeling tighter.

When I first started to understand this concept, an image
popped into my head of a little wall decoration depicting the
cutest little porch with a front door and a roof that I've seen in
the homes of several friends who have traveled to Latin American countries. I thought about that front porch as the entryway
to my soul. When I open the door up for Jesus to come in, where
do I allow him to go?

For the longest time, I was only comfortable letting Jesus in
to a nicely swept little path that I had cleared for him across the
dirty floor. "Here is where you may visit me," I had somehow
communicated to him. "Don't worry about all the other spaces.
You don't really want to go there." I didn't want Jesus to be both-
ered with the mess in the rooms behind the many shut doors
coming off of this area. It was embarrassing and gross and not
worthy of the King of the Universe.

But over time, this idea of real trust in Jesus began to break
through. Here and there, I would open a door, and Jesus would
bring healing and light to that room. Instead of chiding me for
the messiness, he would lovingly help me get it in order. Jesus
wanted to enter every single one of these closed-off rooms, but
he would not force his way in. Once I had the courage to open
that first door, once Jesus proved his healing and transformative
love to me in a dark, lonely place, I began to trust what I had
started to suspect.

Jesus really did want freedom for me, and he was going to
help me get it.

FIVE

CONVERSION

The woman said to him, "Sir, give me this water, so that I may not be thirsty or have to keep coming here to draw water."
—John 4:15

When I started my regular meetings with a spiritual director, Jesus started shining light on my wounds. It was scary. At the front end of this trusting relationship with Jesus, I still needed time to let him prove his love and care for me. I didn't want to face wounds because I didn't know what I would find if I started digging. Pulling back a mask can make you feel vulnerable.

One day, I had a moment of grace. I was doing something quite ordinary, going about my day, and I realized that a memory from my childhood was the root of these feelings of rejection that just would not leave. I had known, deep down, that this memory needed some kind of miraculous healing, but it was so painful for me that I didn't like thinking about it. Asking for prayer from someone trained to deal with inner wounds seemed like a bad idea—I didn't want to "go there," emotionally or mentally. I put off dealing with this for as long as possible.

But this idea of real transformation was a recurring theme. I was thirsty, and Jesus was waiting for me. He wanted to be a part of every area of my life, and that included my past. Like the woman at the well, I had some history that caused me pain. And Jesus was ready to heal me.

Finally, I was ready. I was tired of this memory coming up, tired of having to push those feelings back down, tired of continually having to remind myself that being rejected wasn't who I really was. I was learning to recognize the truth, but the lies continued to present themselves. Also, I knew that this wound had caused some of my problems, my selfishness and negative behavior. It didn't explain every single sin I committed, and it definitely wasn't an excuse, but it sure contributed a lot. It was like a piece of brown cellophane that tinted my vision. It needed to go.

I set up an appointment to get prayers with two women who had been trained in inner healing ministry. In this time of prayer, you talk through the painful memory, and then, in a moment of absolute mystery and goodness, God shines his light on that situation.

This is my painful memory: As a young girl, I had many friends in my neighborhood, and we would play with each other all the time. Every afternoon we would be together, and all day in the summertime these friends were with me outside as we enjoyed our sweet lives as little girls. One day, I found out about a party when a friend asked if I was going. I had not been invited. Not only that, but all my other friends knew about the party and were excited to be going. I don't know why I wasn't invited, but that's not important. What's important is that I didn't know about the party, and everyone else did; everyone else was going, and I was not a part of the excitement.

The smallest thing can sometimes be at the root of great hurt. For years I would tell myself there was no way this memory was the cause of my struggles. How could something so insignificant over the course of a lifetime matter so much? Finally, Jesus showed me that I needed to deal with it. Whether it was the only wound or one of many, this memory caused great pain and suffering for me. It was time to be healed from it.

Heading to my appointment, I was shaking. I entered the home, sat down in a chair surrounded by the women trained in this ministry, and talked through this memory. The details seemed innocent enough, but it wasn't the details that caused the wound. It was the pain of it.

I had tried so long to tell grown-up Rach to just calm down and get over it. *Look how great you are doing in life now!* I would tell myself. *It was a small, insignificant party that you didn't get an invite to. How has it stopped you from having a fabulous life?* No matter what I tried to tell myself, though, little-girl Rachel carried the pain of that rejection. Whether it was intentional or an innocent oversight, it was there, festering and causing problems and feeding me lies whenever it wanted. The pain of that memory had to be acknowledged so it could be released. But I had tried this on my own so many times. How would this be different?

Here's how it was different: After I shared the memory and as the women prayed over me, Jesus came into that memory, and he showed me where he was on that day. All those years ago, as I stood in that open field where we all played together, as I found out about everyone else going to this party, Jesus was standing there beside me. He was with me as I felt rejected and left out. He stood beside me as that wound occurred. He was with me in that sacred pit, standing beside me in my suffering.

Now, here is how human-led healing would take place: My human brain would decide that I was better off without those friends. Or my human brain would tell my heart to just get over it—life goes on. A human choosing how this healing would go could pick a whole host of story lines.

But in that healing moment when Jesus stood beside me and revealed himself to me as I sat in prayer and relived that pain, what happened is that my heart began to swell with over-whelming happiness for my friends. It was the strangest thing. There I was, that little girl watching as her friends shared their excitement about the party she wasn't invited to—and with Jesus standing beside me I was beaming with joy for the fun my friends would have.

I could not believe it.

Instead of the pain being soothed with aloe, it was completely removed. Instead of leaving a scar where the wound had been, the healing left flesh that was healthier than before the wound was inflicted.

Conversion. God made me an offer, I took it, and he began to change everything for me. Jesus was getting into the core of who I was, cleaning up, and making me whole. I trusted him and he was restoring me.

Like the woman at the well, I accepted what Jesus offered— the water that would never run dry—and it changed my life.

I share this experience with you because it proved to me that what God can do for us with his healing love is beyond comprehension. I realized that Jesus has a fullness of spirit and wholeness of heart that can transcend anything my human brain could conjure. And you don't even have to find a healing ministry team. Jesus can enter these wounded areas within us and bring his miraculous healing.

If he could do that for me in this one instant, I wanted him everywhere else with me, too.

Abandonment was scary and life altering. I made an act of courage, and God did the rest.

I can't say that I don't ever struggle with feelings of rejection anymore, but I can tell you that I am no longer afflicted the way I was for so many years. That healing allowed me to see the lies for what they were instead of just believing them. I can now differentiate the truth from the lies. And to the core of my being, I am able to believe the truth.

It's hard to see all that we might gain from this abandonment to Jesus when we are focused on what we might lose. We grow so used to our wounds that we can't imagine living without them.

Similarly, we cling so tightly to our own hopes and dreams, to our own plans, that we are afraid to release the tight grip we have on everything around us. It's exhausting, really, trying to control the universe.

I think about the woman at the well. She showed up that day with her bucket in the middle of her chores, and Jesus was waiting for her. He offered her water that would satiate her deepest thirst—who knew this even existed! When she said yes, she gave Jesus everything, and he transformed her—her past, her present, and her future.

But we can't simply release all of our hopes and dreams and plans to an unknown God. It's not in our nature to be reckless. If we don't really know the living God, how can we entrust our future to him? If we don't know him, we are tempted to think that we need to go with our gut, and everything will work out.

Except that we humans are not the best barometer of wisdom. Sometimes what feels good isn't what is best. Sometimes what makes the most sense in the moment isn't the wisest decision. I once decided a pixie haircut was the best look for my small face. I settled on a plan to surprise everyone (including my husband!) with what surely would be my best haircut ever. Imagine my utter disappointment when I discovered that instead of turning me into a fashionable French film star, short hair made me look more like MacGyver. From the eighties.

Not a wise move. I should have asked for advice. I'm grateful to have learned a valuable lesson at such minimal cost (my personal pride on hold for two years of growing out my hair).

All melodrama aside, what about real issues in our lives? We talk about trust and abandonment to God, handing over everything to him. How do we do that? And how can we be sure we are operating out of wisdom and intellect? Jesus offered the woman at the well a new kind of water. Jesus offered me a new kind of healing. How do we know it is really God's voice we are hearing, and if it's best for us to accept his offer?

Well, as my husband likes to remind me, using the brain God gave us is always a good first step in discernment. Does what I'm considering doing go against my vocation, common sense, or safety? That's a good gauge for whether a decision is good or bad. But with God, we also have to move forward in trust. What God offers is not what the world is selling. We have to decide if we believe in what he says.

Do we believe that the living water Jesus offered the woman—that he offers each one of us—will really leave us satiated? Jesus tells the woman that if she takes the water he offers her, she will no longer be searching. Everything else she might try to quench her thirst with will leave her wanting more, but this water will satisfy her desire.

Do you believe the living water Jesus offers will solve all your problems? Do you trust him with your life?

"Real zeal," wrote Catherine Doherty, "is standing still and letting God be a bonfire in you."[1]

That standing still is what scares us. It's an intense form of abandonment and surrender.

We've been focusing a lot on personal examination and self-analysis; understanding the ups and downs of your interior life is important. But, says Fr. Jacques Philippe in *The Way of Trust and Love*, we can examine this part of our selves too much. If we spend too much time in self-evaluation, we can never be truly satisfied. "Such an attitude causes us to center on ourselves when what we need to do is throw ourselves on God with unlimited trust," he wrote. "The only way really to forget ourselves is by placing all our hope in God."[2]

While we should certainly continue to examine our conscience and consider the state of our interior life, wrote Fr. Philippe, we need to make sure it doesn't become something that causes "discontent and permanent sadness." The antidote for this is to put our gaze on God, "to take his Word as our mirror."[3]

The woman who comes to the well is of this world—she is seeking something of this world to quench her thirst. If she chooses to accept Jesus's offers of living water, she will have to turn away from the world's way of doing business and do things God's way. This is conversion—changing direction.

Conversion is very freeing. It's letting go in trust and surrender in order to finally feel secure. For me, the first step of real conversion was being willing to release my painful memory to Jesus; that encounter brought so much healing that I wanted more. After this initial conversion, we are called to a deeper conversion—a willingness to go deeper with the Lord and give him dominion over every area of our life.

I felt God's desire for me to allow him into more areas of my life. I received him in the Eucharist weekly and sometimes daily and in the Sacrament of Reconciliation. Paul and I prayed with our children every day. We even met once a week with a group of neighbors to pray and encourage each other in our faith lives. But there were still so many areas where I was keeping Jesus out. I had opened one of the doors to him.

Remembering that wall hanging with the miniature steps leading to the porch and the sweet little windows in the little front door that opened in my imagination to a clean hallway filled with mostly closed doors, I realized one day that I was ready to start opening more doors to Jesus.

Why I was hiding from Jesus I couldn't even say. Looking back now, after some moments of grace in this area, it seems very silly. But at the time I was holding on with a very tight fist to certain areas of my life—fears I wasn't willing to release, personal plans I didn't need him getting a hold of, and opinions of others that I somehow felt kept me secure. I thought by giving Jesus access to these areas I would lose something of myself: maybe my plans and hopes and dreams, perhaps even my very sense of self.

God opposes the proud, and he gives his grace to the humble. It is a step in humility to turn our gaze from ourselves to

God. To receive the treasure of the Holy Spirit, the living water, to have the humility and poverty of heart to let go of the areas we try to hold onto in our pride—this is life-changing conversion.

So here's what I decided to do: I was in the habit of spending time in quiet contemplation. But I decided to fully commit to doing this every single day. Each morning I would decide when I would pray that day, and I would commit to praying for 20 minutes. I would even set a timer. This accountability would help me sit longer than what felt comfortable and push through getting distracted and wanting to stop. I fully committed to daily quiet, knowing that there would be times when it wouldn't work out and resolving not to let that fact discouraged me.

One thing that can be scary about silence is having to accept our failings. Modern society makes it easy to stay so plugged in and mentally occupied that we don't have to focus on much at all. When we sit in silence, what might we find? Sitting there and just saying "Hi, Jesus!" was unnerving at first, I'll admit. What if he showed me something bad about myself? That didn't sound like much fun at all.

But over time, I started to recognize my total dependence on the Holy Spirit. I had to be willing to let him into all the areas of my interior life and my day-to-day existence. The more I sat in silence, the more I was willing to open the other doors I had kept shut. I started giving God a chance to be sovereign over each area of my life, and he earned my trust.

It's difficult to accept our limits and weakness, but in this acceptance comes real freedom and deeper conversion. It is no longer about *us* but about *Jesus within us.* Believe it or not, the more time I spent seeking God and listening for his voice, the more I learned to know myself. And as I learned just how good God is, I stopped being so afraid of what he might show me. God is a good Father who wants every good thing for me. Little by little, these truths were opening room after room within my soul.

In this time, I continued meeting with my spiritual director. I grew very committed to spending this time in prayer, and it changed me. It was the living water. I was being transformed.

In conversion, the victories and healings sometimes make it seem as though we will never suffer again. Great strides in virtue should mean I won't ever struggle with this particular sin again, right? Sorry, no—for humans, sin is part of the deal. But we don't have to be controlled by it or be fearful. The good news is that our path to sanctification is not a straight line with a timetable. Knowing that this is all a process should give us real freedom.

My favorite part of this season was God's gentle smile upon me. Even as I was tempted to take myself too seriously in my desire to move forward in personal growth and holiness, God reminded me that he loves me just as I am. In fact, it continues to be a takeaway from my monthly spiritual director meeting that I need to calm my "bad self" down. In focusing on loving God with abandon and working hard to trust him, I sometimes forget he's okay with my humanness. I feel like a failure when I mess up—but then I remember that God says we should never be discouraged by our mistakes. "Hence, now there is no condemnation for those who are in Christ Jesus. For the law of the spirit of life in Christ Jesus has freed you from the law of sin and death" (Rom 8:1–2).

When we sin, we get to thank him for true humility. True humility means being at peace with our brokenness. It's knowing God wants to heal us but also accepting that we are not perfect. Perfection is never a prerequisite for deeper relationship with Jesus.

This tension between pride and humility is the intersection between living life on our own trajectory and being willing to seek fulfillment from something deeper. It's admitting the desire to be extraordinary but allowing God to help you determine what that will be. If our lives are all about our own personal agenda and what we can do with our gifts and skills—even when we think our agenda is about serving the Lord—then it becomes very hard to take our mind off ourselves. Even when we think our focus is something noble—personal growth, doing better and sinning less, being kind to those around us—our focus can be so self-centered that it limits and paralyzes us.

It's also exhausting and pretty boring.

So real freedom and self-knowledge come from quiet intimacy with Jesus. But of course our lives can't be lived entirely in that quiet space. We take our knowledge and deep union with Jesus and go live our life. And Jesus is there too!

Several years ago, I took my children to serve with the Missionaries of Charity for a week at their camp in Atlanta. Henry and Isabel were campers, my big boys served as counselors, and I got to be a "floater," which meant I had a different duty each day. On the last day of camp, we all headed about an hour away to a monastery, where we had Mass and lunch and played games. At one point, all the campers and counselors were off having fun. Finding myself with free time, I quickly headed back into the abbey church to sit in the silence.

I found myself getting very fixated on this silence, almost demanding that God "show up" in a way that I prescribed instead of having a humble, patient visit with a friend. And I clearly heard in the depths of my heart God say to me, "Get up, and go back to the group."

I wanted to feel something spectacular on my terms, but on that day, God wanted me out among his people. It was a good reminder that connection with Jesus is pure gift and that we don't get to control it. I had enjoyed some time in silence, but God let me know that on that day, at that time, it was better for me to be with the group than to be alone for an extended time. Relationship with Jesus should never be all about *me*.

When we take graces from God and use them to feed our egos, God doesn't give us more. The smaller we are, the more we will receive from the Holy Spirit. That's the transformation that conversion brings. We pursue heroic virtue, and we trust that God has us where he wants us in all areas of our lives, including our holiness! We have to be willing to listen to the leading of the Holy Spirit instead of simply assuming we know what God wants to give us and when.

One other big step for me in this conversion was an effort to practice peace. I was tired of feeling stirred up. The inner healing I received was revolutionary, but I still had many habits to rewire. I needed to learn to maintain interior peace by giving all these areas of my life to Jesus. Around this time, I heard a talk encouraging listeners to make little efforts to stay at peace, to not allow troubles to grow within. I needed to shorten my list of grievances, so to speak, and to stop keeping track of who had wronged me and how irked I felt.

Jesus tells us to be of good courage, not to be troubled, that he has overcome the world. Our efforts to remain at peace help us to be open to God's will and the wisdom of the Holy Spirit.

One key concept for me in this season of deeper conversion (which—let's be honest—is an ongoing effort) was detachment. This was a game changer. In the silence, I would find the grace to release things to Jesus that I didn't even realize I clung to.

Several years before this, a friend had given me a set of Catholic self-help audio recordings called *Detaching with Love*. The series, by Fr. Emmerich Vogt, is based on twelve-step programs and addresses the need to establish healthy boundaries and find inner peace. Fr. Emmerich talks a great deal about learning to find Jesus within ourselves and about how our negative interactions with others too often dictate our sense of self-worth. If we allow our interactions with those around us to define who we are, we are held captive by our own thoughts.

With detachment, in contrast, we don't allow those interactions to define us, and it's remarkably freeing. We moves from allowing the things we do to define our worth to allowing who we are and how God sees us to define our worth. Detachment, or freedom from bondage to our fear of what others think of us—good or bad—is also another step toward giving God true control over every area of our life. If we aren't making decisions about our time, money, and career based on what others might think, we are truly free to make these decisions with God.

A life turned toward God, a trusted friend once told me, invokes beauty, joy, and happiness. When I'm looking at God, I will be beautiful and full of joy. When I'm only thinking about myself, I'll be depleted and always needing more—more encouragement, more affirmation, more recognition. The truth of conversion is that when we shift our gaze toward Jesus, we see ourselves as he sees us. We don't need all the accolades because we know who we are in him.

This is absolutely central to Jesus's offer to the woman at the well of water that will never run out. Her happiness and joy won't be contingent on anything that can evaporate; she won't need to keep refilling her bucket, because the source of this refreshment cannot be contained.

Around this time of deeper conversion, I started to consciously seek my identity in Jesus, getting into the habit of asking God to show me who I am in him. Although I knew God loved me, I had never seen myself as a beautiful daughter of God, finding my identity instead in the list of things I was doing. Focusing on how the world might see me was nice when life was exciting and grand. But what about all the other times? It is a dispiriting approach in those seasons when life seems to be moving a lot faster than we are. This must be why God comes to us in these difficult seasons. Unable to continue finding deep satisfaction in our accomplishments, we realize that there has to be more to the truth of our existence—to who we are at our core—than what we are able to do.

It's an easy habit to get into, seeing yourself as the world sees you. Especially if you spend any time on social media, it's easy to think you are the sum of your latest post—the likes, comments, smiley faces, and hearts. Am I clever? Am I funny? Have I said something profound and encouraging lately? What do I have to show for myself?

And of course, there is the bigger picture of what you want to "be" and "do": Will I have an exciting career that will make me seem fabulous? Will I travel and be fascinating? Will I find real meaning and worth in what I do every single day?

But here's what I was learning—none of these things matter to God, as crazy as that sounds. Don't get me wrong. God gives each of us gifts to use, and he really enjoys watching us use these gifts—he delights in us! But what he loves even more is simply us. He loves you. He loves me. Turning our gaze toward Jesus and away from ourselves is the most freeing act of trust and abandonment we can make.

While God wants us to see what we are doing in the moment as what he is asking us to do, he also just wants to love us. He wants us to know we are loved by him. Every so often, my spiritual director once told me, look at Jesus looking back at you with love. This is what time in silence does. It reveals the love of the Father for his beloved. That's me. That's you!

Conversion really is a matter of redirecting our focus. Once I focused on myself; now I focused on Jesus. Once I allowed Jesus into only a few, prepicked areas of my life; now, little by little, I was learning to open the other doors and let him in. Once I thought God wanted to be a part of only preappointed areas of my inner being; now, I started to have proof that he's willing and able to handle it all.

The biggest shift for me came when I made the firm decision to pray every day. Instead of waiting to see where the day would lead me—or treating prayer as an item on my chore list—I committed to making it happen daily. This was easier once I found a form of prayer that was fulfilling, unlike the complaining at God my prayer had once solely been. This doesn't mean my prayer time was no longer about me; now it was about me *and*

God. The two of us. I started asking, boldly, for God to show me I was his beloved.

Perhaps that sounds selfish, but in order for me to more fully trust in God and his great plan for my life, I had to learn to know and receive his love. The best way to do that, it seemed to me, was to plop down somewhere quiet and just show up.

So I did that.

And while God was showing up in deep, powerful ways for me in prayer, my "real" life was also expanding. Enough had shifted at home that I could work teaching journalism at the local university—a dream job that fell in my lap after I noticed a need for adjuncts in my field while on the university website looking for a work-study program for our son Elliott. I was hired full-time within a year through very little effort on my part.

By now—and here is the really wonderful thing—I could see this job as a gift from God instead of something to add to a list of personal credentials to stroke my ego. I'm proud of my accomplishments—don't get me wrong—but as much as I absolutely love this job, I don't use it to soothe that deep ache I felt earlier.

One of the biggest blessings of this job is that there's an adoration chapel right across the street from my office. Once I started working full-time, I made daily adoration part of my routine; I committed to stopping by every day on my way to class to sit in silence for twenty minutes. This went on for several years and is what allowed God to keep making changes in me.

During the pandemic, I decided not to allow myself to backslide. If the adoration chapel was closed, I would create the next best thing—a quiet prayer space in our home. The place that worked was inside our walk-in closet, which is literally a walk-in—no extra space in there beyond the little runway on the floor that divides my side from Paul's. But it was big enough to fit a small prayer rug Paul brought back from a business trip to Turkey and a small plant stand that was the perfect mini altar, just big enough for a candle and a crucifix.

In this season, I would decide each morning on a time for my silent prayer that day. That it would happen was nonnegotiable; the timing I was willing to be flexible on. Whatever worked for that day—morning, midmorning, or afternoon—was more important than having a set time that I couldn't always make work. I would set a timer and enter my prayer chamber, which turned out to be quite practical, as people were less likely to disturb me there.

But this prayer chamber also became a sacred space within me where only God and I could dwell. A friend once described this quiet inner focus of prayer like this: Deep inside each one of us is a place where the Blessed Trinity dwells. The Father, Son, and Holy Spirit are there inside you, waiting to spend time with you.

For me, turning to silence was truly transformative. There was still a time and place for intercession, going to God in earnest request for my needs, but I was finding solace and healing in the silence, in seeking connection with God and experiencing his deep love for me.

It didn't take long for the peace to be evident. The good work had been started with miraculous healing, and it continued with this silence. In prayer, I started to hear truth instead of lies, love instead of rejection. My peace and joy came not from feeling accepted by everyone around me but from leaning into God's love and grace.

Psalm 63 expresses this experience perfectly:

O God, you are my God—
    it is you I seek!
For you my body yearns;
    for you my soul thirsts,
In a land parched, lifeless,
    and without water.
I look to you in the sanctuary
    to see your power and glory.

For your love is better than life;
    my lips shall ever praise you!
I will bless you as long as I live;
    I will lift up my hands, calling on your name.
My soul shall be sated as with choice food,
    with joyous lips my mouth shall praise you!
I think of you upon my bed,
    I remember you through the watches of the night
You indeed are my savior,
    and in the shadow of your wings I shout for joy.
My soul clings fast to you;
    your right hand upholds me. (1–9)

Jesus tells the woman at the well that the things of this world will not quench her thirst like the water he has to offer. This is the life-changing concept: that what Jesus has to offer is better and more fulfilling than what the world offers us. We get a small taste of the victory the world says will bring us true happiness—and we quickly want and need more. With Jesus, we will be satiated.

But only a deep relationship with Jesus will fill us. Not even doing noble deeds for Jesus is the real relationship that our soul seeks. Only in the stillness of our soul can we find this deep union with God where true, deep conversion can take place.

It takes effort. It takes a willingness to recognize the pain and wounds we feel and then not spend too much time focusing on them. It requires opening those doors within our soul that need tending by God. It requires a real letting go and asking God to lead us to the quiet waters that will restore our soul.

Before I get too carried away in my poetic tales of deeper conversion, let me say this: it's an ongoing process, a path that winds and bends and loops back around. I know the truth, and it is indeed setting me free. There are times when grand change happens and times when it's a gentle, subtle shift.

Being a human is part of the deal. God can live with our limits because he created us to be humans with our human limitation. I sometimes want to pray and seek God's love and solace in such a way as to ensure I won't have human emotions and feelings anymore. If I'm properly tapped into the Lord's flowing grace, I'll be able to rise above the temptation to be discouraged. Right?

But this just isn't reality. We pray; we seek God's voice; we pursue holiness and deeper conversion. We work hard to focus on ourselves just enough to understand how God is using our life circumstances to draw us closer to him. And then we stop that self-focus and turn our gaze to Jesus. Real freedom comes from this perspective.

The circumstances that led me to Jesus were my feelings that life was passing me by. Back when I sat in that theater and cried watching *Moana*, what was I feeling? I was experiencing the deep longing my soul had for something more than just status quo. My soul was thirsting for more than what this world has to offer.

I'm so glad I didn't take the offer the world makes—to have more in your life through an acute focus on your life circumstances. This water the world offers will never truly satisfy. If I try to use my here and now as the source for abiding joy and deep satisfaction, I will have to keep coming back to the well to refill. Again and again and again.

Jesus offers us living water that will never run dry. If we are smart, we take advantage of these streams he offers. And we need them because we are sinners and humans who suffer from our sin and fallen nature.

Jesus walks beside us in the midst of it, as we humbly ask him to guide us and lead us and give us the grace to hear his voice.

SIX

SURRENDER

Jesus said to her, "Go, call your husband, and
come back." The woman answered him, "I have
no husband."

—John 4:16–17

The woman at the well takes Jesus up on his offer. She trusts him
and accepts. And once she's decided to abandon herself to Jesus,
he acknowledges her sin, saying, "Go, call your husband and
come back." And the woman, in that moment, surrenders. She
can't pretend she has a husband. She doesn't act like she didn't
hear Jesus. "I have no husband," she admits. She has decided to
let God be in charge. She is no longer in control, and this is the
best decision she has ever made.

We try so hard to control so many things. And we think it
defines us. We choose our career and our job, how we spend our
time and where we go. And all of these things, we falsely believe,
are who we are. They are not.

You are not what you do. You are not your job or your volunteer work. You are not your latest success; you are not your latest
failure. The core of who you are is not how well your marriage
is going or whether you've found the right person to marry. It's
not the latest agitation at work, but neither is it the latest award.

Your worth does not come from whether you've pinpointed
the thing in life that gets you the most excited, whether you are
crushing it in your home decorating goals, or whether you've

perfectly executed a career shift that's going to make you happy and free. None of these are the nucleus of your being.

Surrender is about starting to look at yourself not from the outside in but from the inside out. Surrender is a major paradigm shift, not a quick transformation. It's a willingness to see things in a completely new light, and that takes time.

When we view ourselves from the inside out, we don't have to look through the lens of worldly success and achievement. And how do we shift our gaze? By learning to hear the quiet, still voice of the one who loves us more than we can ever hope to understand. Worldly success and achievement are not bad things, but we sell ourselves short and are always at the mercy of our most recent success or failure when that's where we look.

The woman at the well considers Jesus's offer of the living water; she has to decide if she's willing to give it a try. It's a new concept for her. Could it possibly be that this man, waiting for her in her daily duties, can really solve all her problems? Will she no longer be searching for the thing her soul knows is missing? She didn't see this coming. She didn't expect this to be the solution.

I wanted to feel happier inside, wanted my life to feel exciting. The solution was revealing itself to me, and it wasn't what I expected.

Surrender is getting to the point where you are willing to see yourself in a different light. Could it be that my career, my ambitions, my hopes and dreams, and my family are not the things that define me or give me true, deep abiding joy? Could it be that holding tight to my past hurts and agitations does not make me feel more secure?

These are challenging, confusing questions. All of these moving parts of our lives—our abilities, our talents, our loved ones—are good things, and every good thing comes from God. So why wouldn't we see ourselves as deeply connected to all of this goodness?

What happens if we aren't careful, however, is that our identity becomes wrapped up in these things. Instead of just really loving our job, we derive our worth from how our job is going. Instead of just deeply loving our spouse, we are somehow a reflection of how strong (or weak) our marriage is.

This is where things can break down. When we derive a false sense of security in these areas, we run the risk of allowing our self-worth to be at the mercy of the externals of our life. Are you a truly wonderful person only if your marriage is truly wonderful? Are you a truly happy person only if you are advancing at a reasonable rate in your career? Are you a fulfilled mother only if you still have children dependent on you?

If my life is going well, does that mean I'm a better person? Does my worth come from the things I do? If what I'm doing isn't noticeable, doesn't it have less worth? Is my happiness and fulfillment contingent on my going after my dreams and getting whatever it is my heart desires? What if I'm happy just making it through the day? Does that mean I'm lame?

These were questions I had to ask myself because of my situation. When Henry and Isabel came on the scene, I was barely making it through the day. If I was judging myself based on how well I was managing my life, I was not going to get high marks. My life circumstances were challenging, I was not crushing it, and I no longer wanted that to dictate my self-worth.

I was hearing a lot of talk about going after your dreams, crushing that vision board, making things happen, and not being trapped by the confines of your daily existence. Except I was totally trapped. I didn't hate it, but I definitely was not in a position to make major changes like applying for a new graduate program or starting a new career. I couldn't even make it to a middle school basketball game. I had outsourced (to my husband) the job of cheering on my boys because taking a rambunctious three-year-old to a gym for the fourth night in a row was more than I could handle.

I wasn't exactly a woman who had the energy to reinvent herself. I just wanted a nap. Although the things I was doing were keeping me plenty busy, they were not exactly what I would call "lifelong dreams."

But strange as it may seem, hitting this level of burnout was forcing me to surrender—to give up what I had always considered real success and adventure and find peace from a new, other, much deeper source.

The transformative time in quiet was healing my soul, and I was also beginning to trust that where I was, right here in this moment, was where Jesus wanted me to be. The grand, loftier ambitions I had weren't going to happen right this minute. More than any of those, I just wanted to be happy and at peace. And I was starting to embrace the concept that my self-worth didn't need to come from going off and doing amazing things. I still had amazing things I wanted to do, but it wasn't happening right this minute.

Maybe fabulous adventure was on hold, but that didn't mean my personal happiness had to be on hold.

In the divide between what I was doing with my life and what I thought were my hopes and dreams, something really strange was happening: I was finding true happiness and fulfillment from a new source—my yes to Jesus in the duty of the moment.

But also, my true happiness was starting to come from something deeper. The change got my attention because I didn't see it coming.

It was the most drowning season of my life, when it was all I could do to try to keep up with two small children and four bigger boys. The volunteer work and speaking and writing were all on hold—I just couldn't swing it. I wasn't even getting personal props from being a turbo mom who could do everything for her kids. All I could manage was the life inside our home, which was not how I tended to see the world. Until then, I had been happiest with an outward view, with a focus on the next thing I would tackle that might get me noticed.

But now, I felt happy and satisfied just to switch over the laundry and get little people to bed. I had peace and felt joy, but not because I knew one day those grand opportunities would come back or because there was something on the calendar to look forward to. It was because, little by little, I was starting to believe Jesus's offer: that if I was willing to use the living water he offered to quench my thirst, then he would give me deep, fulfilling satisfaction. The surrender that follows conversion—shifting my sense of self-worth from what I did to who God made me to be—was changing me.

This simple time in prayer was doing big things. It felt miraculous.

How in the world, I wondered, *can spending time in quiet contemplation be any kind of substitute for all the things I'm hearing will bring me real happiness?*

All the stories we hear of adventure and dreaming big dreams inspire us to want more for our lives. They tell us we can't be satisfied with mediocrity, with settling for less. It didn't make sense that this stirring deep within me could point toward letting go of wanting more. The two concepts seemed at odds with one another.

I returned to the Holy Father's words all those years earlier at World Youth Day: "It is Jesus in fact that you seek when you dream of happiness; he is waiting for you when nothing else you find satisfies you; he is the beauty to which you are so attracted; it is he who provokes you with that thirst for fullness that will not let you settle for compromise; it is he who urges you to shed the masks of a false life; it is he who reads in your hearts your most genuine choices, the choices that others try to stifle."[1]

Are adventure and achievement masks of a false life? These things aren't bad, but what if making them the goal, ranking them higher than our interior life with God, creates the false life?

I don't want to live a false life. I don't want to be searching in the wrong place, spending my time and energy trying to fill my cup—the deepest recesses of my soul—with a water that will never satisfy. I don't want to keep coming back for more of something that can't fill the hole in my being that only Jesus can fill.

We were made for more—but that "more" comes from deep inside us rather than from an external source. More freedom and joy and absolute bliss come not from searching outward but from seeking and finding that sacred space deep within our spirit where Jesus sits and waits to be found. That place in our souls where the Blessed Trinity can connect with us. That deep connection will meet every single other need you might have in your life.

This dive into the sacred space inside is the truest adventure because it casts off every false self—the self that wants to be affirmed and noticed, the self that wants to do the right thing and be the best version of itself. The sacred space is where Jesus meets you and says, "None of that matters." He is bigger than whatever sadness and hurt and failure you have experienced.

We yearn for more than this daily existence has to offer because God created our soul for more than the things of this world. "It is Jesus who stirs in you the desire to do something great with your lives," St. John Paul II continued, "the will to follow an ideal, the refusal to allow yourselves to be ground down by mediocrity, the courage to commit yourselves humbly and patiently to improving yourselves and society, making the world more human and more fraternal."[2]

I want to make the world more human and more fraternal. I want to improve myself and society. I don't want to be ground down by mediocrity. Also, I want to make it through the day in this place right here, the place God seems to see fit to have me. Do I trust him with my hopes and dreams? With my personal happiness?

Until I started connecting with him in contemplative prayer, I believed that true happiness meant following my dreams. Now I was starting to see that true happiness meant letting go of trying to control every aspect of my life. True peace meant giving God reign over every single one of my hopes and dreams, my vision for how to spend my time and energy.

It was a circle. Following my dreams meant giving them to God, trusting that he could dream bigger than I ever could. It meant knowing that if God had placed within me a real desire for happiness and adventure, then he would guide me in getting there.

In the meantime, there's the daily grind. You know what I'm talking about. I've said a lot of lofty stuff about feeling fulfilled and having dreams. Then there's the reality of dealing with your actual life, the one that's still going to be there waiting for you whether you find the perfect career or decide to glamp your way along the Appalachian Trail.

Wherever you go, there you are.

This is an amazing part of the water that will truly satisfy: God is so much smarter than we are. We see ourselves in these little boxes—Adventure Rach, Mama Rach, Wifey Rach, Amazing Motivational Speaker Rach—while God sees just one Rach. And he sees that that one Rach needs some ways to make life rich and peaceful and happy, most notably by slowing down. Because staying on the go does not make our problems go away.

When you slow down and sit in silent contemplation, you have to face some stuff. That can be scary. I didn't want to sit and be quiet only to think about all my failures. I didn't want to have this overwhelming focus on all the times my wounded self has wounded others. I didn't want to fixate on my sinfulness. That's not fun at all.

Our awesome God, though, really can handle all those things. And when we are willing to face them—in the quiet of our hearts, with a trusted friend, with a wise mentor—we get the healing we need to move forward in freedom. We give these areas over to God and let him show us how to proceed.

Fr. Mike Schmitz talks about surrender as giving God "access." This is a mind-blowing concept. Sometimes we think of surrendering something to God as wanting him to take it away. We surrender a situation to God and expect him to just come in and obliterate it. (For good or bad, I tend to think this way.) "Lord, I surrender everything to you" can feel like code for "Take it away or fix it right this minute, please."

Or as we say in the South, "Jesus, take the wheel."

This is why the concept of surrender can be so scary. What if I don't want God to just vaporize this part of my life? If I surrender it to Jesus, he might do something crazy! If I surrender my marriage to him, what does that mean? If I surrender my kids to him, will he really care for them as much as I do? If I surrender my hopes and dreams for the future and for right this minute, will God make things boring?

But what if, as Fr. Mike says, we simply give God access to all these areas?

Let's consider it. If we give God access to our entire life—the impossible situations, the everyday agitations, the pure joy and absolute heartache—we give him lordship over them all, which starts to yield real freedom. We are loosening our tightly clenched fists. We aren't tossing these things away; we are welcoming God into the center of them.

"It's not mine to claim; it's the Lord's now," says Fr. Mike. In surrendering, we give the Lord access to our relationships with our family, with our friends, with our children. And we give God access to our hopes and dreams.

I could never have believed any of this a decade ago. Only after I accepted God's healing and love and learned to trust in his great plan for my life could I even consider giving him "access." Before this, I could not have released my hold on my life. But giving him access to it all is freeing.

Most importantly, when I give God access to my brokenness, to my woundedness, I have found that real miracles can start to happen.

An early result was a very subtle shift in my thinking. Now the little story I'll share might sound like a silly example, but my aim is to show you how deep God can get into our being if we give him access. It was proof to me that in response to my opening up my inner poverty to him, Jesus was making some changes to my core beliefs.

As I mentioned earlier, I had always struggled with feelings of rejection even though I have lots of friends and know I'm loved. It was so frustrating that I believed this nagging lie that I wasn't accepted even though I could clearly see its falsehood. It was a tiny root in my heart that I felt helpless to overcome. I was not able to have victory in this area until I started, in prayer, to open that little space to Jesus, to offer it to him instead of keeping it hidden.

Of course, even though I had tried to hide this brokenness from him, God already saw it and already loved me. We don't reach out to God for healing because we need him to love us more; Jesus doesn't want to heal us so he can find us more lovable. That's impossible—he literally could not love us any more than he already does. He sees the brokenness and wounds, and he still loves us.

But if we want freedom from our brokenness and wounds, God is willing to give it to us, and he wants that for us. Perhaps there will be no instant healing; perhaps a particular wound is something we will struggle with for the rest of our lives. St. Paul, we read in 2 Corinthians, had a "thorn in the flesh" (12:7) that God never removed; whatever it was, God decided St. Paul needed to keep it. But when we give Jesus access to every area of our life, we no longer have to carry our burdens on our own. Perhaps a particular burden won't leave us, but God will lighten this load and we will see, in some small way, that he is using it to draw us closer to himself or, as he did with St. Paul, to show his power within us.

For me it was exhausting, always walking around with this low-grade feeling of not fitting in. It didn't control me most of the time, but I was constantly aware of it and sometimes had to work very hard to overcome it. When the initial healing happened, it changed so much, but I still had so many faulty ways of thinking that had to be retrained.

I started offering this brokenness to Jesus, showing and releasing it to him. "I don't love this about myself," I told God, "and I also don't totally understand it." But although I had some good conversations about it with my spiritual director that helped me gain some freedom, this strange core belief—that I was a junior varsity player in a varsity world—remained.

Then one day I walked into a favorite store and said a hearty hello to the greeter. This person answered with little enthusiasm. No big deal; I was happy enough for the both of us (Hooray for dish towel shopping and looking at purses!). A while later, as I was checking out, I noticed this same greeter say hello to an incoming shopper with a little more vigor. And this was my thought: *My kindness to that person helped them be kind to someone else.*

The old Rachel, who suffered so much from feelings of rejection, would have thought something more like, *Of course that person would be friendlier to someone else. You never get treated with that much kindness. You don't deserve the same kind of friendliness, I guess.* Cue a weird, very subtle downward spiral.

But on that day, walking out of the store, instead of seeing myself as the person who was treated with less kindness, I saw a person whose kindness helped inspire someone else. It wasn't prideful—not like, you're so amazing you just make the world full of *joy*, Rachel!—but an ability to see myself as part of something positive. It was a total shift in my thinking, in my view of myself, and in my view of the world around me.

God did that for me. It was simple and also truly profound. I was excited to find out what else God could do if I continued to surrender and trust that life with Jesus at the core could be worth more than anything the world has to give.

We all have areas of suffering from wounds and lies that Jesus really wants to heal. Yours might not be rejection. Maybe it's fear of being wrong, or fear of abandonment. Maybe you struggle with comparison, or the wounds of growing up in a broken home. Our human frailty leaves us as the walking wounded. And God wants to heal us and give us freedom.

SEVEN

HEALING THROUGH TRUTH

The woman said to him, "I know that the Messiah is coming, the one called the Anointed; when he comes, he will tell us everything." Jesus said to her, "I am he, the one who is speaking with you."
—John 4:25–26

The woman knows someone is coming who has all the answers. Could this man at the well be him? Jesus tells her he is the Anointed One: the very person she is speaking to right now is the one she has been waiting for.

Deep within us, we too know that there is more to life than this way I'm living, this way I think—this can't be all there is.

We love stories of transformation. Many of the saints had stories of dramatic change. God bless St. Monica, who prayed for her son Augustine for thirty years. What faith! I always ask God to spare me having to have that much faith—I want things done now! There is St. Teresa of Avila, known for her excessive chattiness, who learned how to lean into God's quiet voice and find the wisdom and virtue she needed to become a holy woman. Her example has transformed many lives. One of my favorite inspirations is St. Paul. He set out on his horse, and by the time he hit the ground partway through his trip, he was someone totally different. Saul to Paul, in a flash.

We have a print of Caravaggio's *The Conversion of Saint Paul* hanging in our kitchen, a gift from Fr. Tim, who lived in Rome during seminary and then several years later as a spiritual director at the same seminary. In this image, Saul/Paul is on the ground. His horse looms over him, and in the dark, shadowy background, a man stands looking down. Most of the light in this painting is on Paul's chest. His eyes are closed, and his arms reach ramrod straight in the air, his hands open wide.

He has been transformed through his encounter with the truth of Jesus. He is not the same, and he will never be the same again. God has had his way with Paul.

Jesus is the great healer. He wants to heal us, and he can do it. How many of us go to the doctor ready to tell the doctor what is wrong with us? Truthfully, most of us. We show up, having already googled our symptoms, with a strong sense of exactly what the problem is and how it needs to be fixed. Most of the time, I find out that the problem is much less horrific than my googling led me to believe.

Too often it is the same with Jesus. We show up ready to tell him our personal assessment of what needs to be fixed: "Heal me, Jesus, in the following, very specific ways." But once we surrender and give Jesus access, once we learn to trust him so that we can release our hold on all these areas, the Lord can do wonders.

I've mentioned before that almost every time I meet with my spiritual director, my takeaway is that things are much less mangled than I previously thought. The devil loves to keep us in bondage. He uses the past to condemn us and the future to cause fear and anxiety.

Great healing begins when we allow God into these sacred, wounded areas. He climbs down into the sacred pit with us, stands beside us, and shines his perfect, healing light on these areas. Sometimes this healing requires therapy; sometimes it takes the kind of inner healing I experienced. I've had healing moments in confession and in personal prayer. Jesus will use all of these tools to get us healed and whole.

The woman at the well lets God shine his healing light in her life by owning the truth of her past. She has had five husbands (see John 4:17–19), and still Jesus offers her the living water. Jesus is not afraid of her past. Because Jesus is not put off by her sins, the woman is transformed by his living water. She is no longer defined by the mistakes she's made, by the suffering she has endured. She is a new woman who goes out and tells the town about what Jesus did for her.

Many of us may feel that our story is not this radical. We didn't have to be knocked off a horse the way St. Paul did; we don't have multiple ex-husbands and all the baggage that brings.

But we all have a past. We have hurts that we've incurred in our human journey. Things are said and done that latch onto us. Some remain gaping wounds. Some stick around as scar tissue; the sting is gone, but something remains that impacts how we see the world around us.

Truly, the Lord says to each one of us, I want to heal you.

When God calls us to deeper union with him, he teaches us our true identities as his beloved children. This process takes time, but the healing is real.

I knew in theory that I was beloved by God, but I could not understand it deep within me. I was still caught up in the lies that who I was depended entirely on what I did, that I was what I did. I was Rachel Balducci, wife, mama, newspaper columnist, speaker, author, and college teacher! It was great to have so many wonderful accomplishments next to my name—an honor and a privilege to have this vocation and do these great things (for Jesus!). But I was attaching my self-worth and identity to these things. Who was I without them? Honestly, a nobody.

Aren't we all nobodies when you take away the externals? Except we aren't. We are very much somebodies—we are children of God.

If this sounds trite to you, I get it. For the longest time, being a child of God just didn't make sense to me. What did it even mean? My mind immediately wandered to the cover of Ethan's Catholic baby book—beautiful gold lettering and a sweet little sketched cherub on the cover. Child of God sounded perfect for a newborn baby. But how could it be enough for grown-up me?

And yet I was thirsty for more. Here and there, I had experienced the thrill of adventure, and it was wonderful. But it was not enough. Even though I had tasted so much goodness in my external identities, they didn't fill the God-sized hole in my heart.

A screeching halt was an excellent way to reset my identity. If I was the sum of my current parts, where did that leave me? And if the best thing I had going was being a mama (which was pretty amazing!), where would that leave me in a few years when my children were grown and gone?

Through God's grace, I started seeking answers in silence, the halt my busy life needed. "God is the friend of silence," said St. Teresa of Calcutta. In that silence, God brought healing. Most times in prayer, I was just aware of God's presence. Sometimes God shined his healing light on a sad memory or an agitation. Oftentimes I felt peace and later in the day would have the wisdom and words to deal with a tricky situation without asking God specifically for them.

One of the most profound healings came almost imperceptibly. There were so many relationships in my life where I wanted to be affirmed. It was exhausting, really. The friendships I struggled with the most were with people who seemed to have it more "together" than I did. As a mama with five sons, I never felt like I had my act together. I wanted to be someone who had well-behaved children, especially at Mass and other public places, and tended to be jealous of anyone who was "winning" in that regard.

One day, leaning hard into my vocation as mother, I took my five sons to adoration at our gigantic, marble-clad church with acoustics that won't quit. As we made our way to the front of the church, the Blessed Sacrament was on the altar and other people were soaking up the sacred silence. Just as the last of the five boys found a spot in the front pew, a small skirmish broke out between two of them. It was loud, and everything echoed. By the time I rose from genuflecting, it was time to exit right. Quickly.

We headed back down the aisle toward the exit as I fought back tears, devastated. What kind of Catholic mama can't even bring her kids to adoration?

This one.

After releasing my bigger hopes and dreams to God, I still needed to give him the small things. My identity as a mother wouldn't supply the deeper peace that only God can give.

I wanted to be holy, good, and free of selfish clinging. I wanted to dominate with goodness and virtue. I felt so far away from all of these things.

If I had googled my symptoms and walked in to the Great Healer with my diagnosis and cure, I would have said something like, "Please help my children behave better. Help me obey you perfectly. Help me hear your voice and your perfect plan, and help all the areas in my life fall into place better than I ever could have dreamed." To be honest, I think I spent years praying some form of that prayer. "Help me to be good. Help me to be lovable. Help me to parent perfectly, and give me the right words always."

Instead, God went way deeper, piercing the surface of that prayer to heal me deeply so that I didn't need every area of my life to feel perfect. He healed my heart and my view of myself. He healed my overactive need for affirmation and my need for perfection. He brought me great peace and the knowledge that part of being a human is human nature. He doesn't need me to be perfect. He just wants to love me.

If I had had my way, God would have healed me on my terms with a bandage. None of what I wanted fixed really mattered—it was all surface-level stuff to make the outside look better, shinier, so that I could feel better about my little world.

Perhaps the woman at the well expected water from Jesus that had to be refilled only once a week instead of daily. Maybe she would have settled for a servant to go fetch the water for her. Instead, God met her more profoundly than any solution she could have conjured.

God healed me in ways it didn't occur to me to ask for. He showed me that he loved me so I didn't need as much affirmation from others. He healed my need for perfection so that when my children messed up, I didn't worry (quite as much!) what others thought. He healed my brokenness so that I could love myself in spite of messing up.

These flaws are not eradicated, but I can assure you that what used to feel like giant roadblocks now feel like hiccups. Negative interactions that used to leave me laid out on the ground in need of resuscitation now feel like little bruises.

God gave me perspective and a willingness to see myself the way he sees me—as beloved. Reading several of the Dutch priest, theologian, and prolific spiritual writer Henri Nouwen's books was life changing for me. "Self-rejection," he wrote in *Life of the Beloved*, "is the greatest enemy of the spiritual life because it contradicts the sacred voice that calls us the 'Beloved.' Being the Beloved expresses the core truth of our existence."[1]

God wants us to know we are beloved by him, that this is the core of our identity. We can only know this identity in the quietest spaces of our hearts. Until we lean into our true identity as beloved children of God, we will look to externals for our identity and for love. *If I am treated with love, I am loved*, we think. *If am treated cruelly, perhaps I am not worthy of being loved.*

It didn't take much for this way of thinking to take root in me, even though I was raised by loving parents. The oldest of eight children, I have many memories of growing up in a home filled with love and joy. And yet a few negative interactions along the way stuck to me: being left out as a young girl, having fun poked at me by older kids, being the slowest at recess, the last to be picked for kickball.

For years I felt trapped in my negative emotions but also helpless to change anything. It wasn't until God started drawing me in to himself that change began. I gave God access to these sad memories and asked him to heal me. And he did. As he did with the woman at the well, God offered me something deeper and better than the human brain can imagine—a miracle. God's plans are way better than ours.

Years ago, a science center in our town featured a kugel fountain, a giant spherical stone resting on a hollowed-out pedestal. The stone is usually too heavy for humans to lift, but once water begins to fill the tiny space between stone and pedestal, a small child can spin it forward and backward. Without the water, even a team of strong men is helpless to move the stone.

So it is with the Holy Spirit, with Jesus and his miraculous healing. Things that seem impossible for men are easily accomplished by God (see Luke 18:27). God can do big things for us, without very much effort on our part, because he is the living water that is doing much of the work.

This healing doesn't happen because we deserve it or because we earn it. It isn't about becoming holy enough to properly receive God's love. It is about believing and accepting his offer.

Tired, putting off a task, and already feeling behind in life, I hopped on my favorite social media platform one morning to scroll. (I make the mistake a little too often of using social media to distract me when I need a break from my actual priorities.)

As I looked at picture after picture, I noticed a growing feeling of restlessness in my spirit. The images and videos made me feel small rather than happy. Instead of being inspired, I felt defeated.

One friend's book award felt like a threat. Another friend's viral comedy video made me feel left in the dust. There was the person who had a priest over to celebrate the Feast of the Sacred Heart. *Why didn't I think of that?* I asked myself. *That was a really good idea.*

Everyone else's gain felt like my loss. They were winning; I was not. Everything seemed grand and accomplished, and there I stood hunched over my kitchen island, phone in hand, putting off my reality.

Reality. That was the word I needed to hear. These images were not the sum of reality. They were snippets of victory for people I really care about. But I was comparing those tidbits of their lives, small moments of great joy to be sure, to the whole of my life. Comparing their external to my internal, I was feeling churned up and spit out.

Those negative feelings were a sign that something in my spirit was off. But I didn't need to change my to-do list for the day to keep up with these wonderful women. In fact, the picture of the priest saying Mass for that feast day prompted the question that ultimately provided an answer. *I didn't think of that,* I finally told myself, *because that's not who I am.*

It's not who I am. It's not where I'm at. This isn't a bad thing. It's just the truth. I did not think up the words that filled that award-winning book or the humor in the funny video or the idea to invite a priest over to celebrate the Feast of the Sacred Heart because that's not where God has me. That's not who I am.

For the longest time, comparing my life and accomplishments with those of others would send me into a spiral. I would see someone else's victory and feel threatened by it. I would wish I had thought of it first, wish I had the energy or desire or cleverness to do business the way that person does business. I would get so focused on what the other person had going on that I would lose sight of who I was, who God made me to be.

Social media is just one arena where comparison becomes the thief of joy. There are so many opportunities in life to be trucking along feeling really good about things and then, *Bam!*, we hear about someone else's victory and feel deflated. Someone else's job advancement, someone else's award at work. The college someone's child got into. The faster runner, the faster swimmer. Others will so often succeed in ways that look different from our own success.

If we walk around looking too much at all the externals around us, we set ourselves up for lots of time spent feeling "less than." We feel only as good as our latest victory, only as happy as our latest successful endeavor. It's a temptation many of us have that leaves us living in a tiny little world of petty comparison. Instead of being aware of the goodness in our own life, we are hyperaware of the goodness everyone else has.

Now, not everyone really struggles with this, or perhaps we all struggle with it to varying degrees. God bless those awesome people who never feel threatened! My husband is always so amazed when I'm tempted to care too much about what's going on with those around me. "I'm just so happy to be me," he usually jokes, "that none of that other stuff matters." Being aware of the goodness others have isn't a bad thing if we have a good sense of who we are—the truth of our very personal, one-on-one relationship with Jesus.

Paul is a great example of how we are supposed to operate. His outlook isn't pride; it's freedom in truth. And it's evidence of God's truth acting in Paul's life. God made each one of us; we are wonderfully made, as the psalmist reminds us. God wants us to be aware of this great gift and the depths to which our Creator knows us:

> You formed my inmost being;
>   you knit me in my mother's womb.
> I praise you, because I am wonderfully made;
>   wonderful are your works!
>   My very self you know.
> My bones are not hidden from you,

When I was being made in secret,
    fashioned in the depths of the earth.
Your eyes saw me unformed;
    in your book all are written down;
    my days were shaped, before one came to be. (Ps 139:13–16)

As candid as I'm being about my struggle, there has been great healing for me in this area. What used to take days to get over, and involved several phone calls to my mom or my husband or trusted friends, now presents as a mere temptation to get in a funk. It takes me a minute to recognize that I'm focusing on the wrong thing, and I get some perspective pretty quick.

The biggest advancement for me in this area is true, deep understanding of God's love for me to the core, knowing who I am in Jesus, and beginning to accept that my worth does not come from any of these temporal achievements. I am not the sum of what I do. I am not the highs and lows of my day-to-day existence.

This is certainly not to diminish any of the awesome things I saw that morning on social media. In fact, it helps me celebrate others' success even more. While I might be tempted, when I'm in a vulnerable spot, to get caught up in comparison, a quick reset reminds me of what life is really all about and helps me feel free to love and celebrate the beauty and success of those around me.

But we can only do this when our understanding of Truth is on a firm foundation.

I remember years ago watching a press conference with a disgraced politician caught cheating on his wife. He described his indiscretion as being his truth—"my truth," he called it. My truth. Not *the* truth. And that's the trend now, an attitude that truth is very personal and personalized. There is no one truth that fits all. We all now get *our* truth.

So, morality police aside, let's go with that terminology. Absolute truth exists, and it's what we need as a firm foundation for a happy life. It's freeing to know there is Truth outside of the many variables of the human condition. Having said that, if you would like to have your own personal truth, here it is: *your* truth is that you have a God who loves you to the core of your being. You have a God who sees you beyond your latest victory and your latest defeat. You have a God who sees you so clearly and loves you so fiercely that all the other details in your life pale in comparison to the burning desire Jesus has for *you*.

Your truth is that no matter what struggle you are facing, God is bigger. No matter what hurt you are experiencing, God is vaster. He is deeper and wider and higher and in it and around it. In comparison to the Truth of God, you have nothing to fear.

What a truth you have! What victory we gain in dwelling on that truth and living in that truth. God knows everything about us and is pleased with us.

> LORD, you have probed me, you know me:
> you know when I sit and stand;
> you understand my thoughts from afar.
> You sift through my travels and my rest;
> with all my ways you are familiar.
> Even before a word is on my tongue,
> LORD, you know it all.
> Behind and before you encircle me
> and rest your hand upon me.
> Such knowledge is too wonderful for me,
> far too lofty for me to reach. (Ps 139:1–6)

Down deep, our souls know this truth. That's why we feel it when we are searching for peace and happiness in a place where we won't find it. God doesn't want us to settle for mediocrity; he knows we won't find deep happiness from the externals of our life.

We will find *some* satisfaction and happiness and joy from externals. Those are nice things and will not be bad for us. But they are like the bucket that must be filled again and again. It will be a nice drink, but it will leave us needing more.

Searching within ourselves to find God and taking the living water offered by Jesus will quench this thirst. It will fill us up, each one of us very personally, so that the externals of the world around us will no longer feel like a threat. We will have the freedom to celebrate all the goodness in this world, including the goodness others have, without seeing it as something we don't get.

Of course we are humans and will have human struggles. The point of going deeper in prayer, of quenching our thirst with living water, is not to become robots who never have human emotions. As much as I want prayer to make me impervious to the human condition, that's not how God made us to be.

But he understands this, and he wants to offer us the perspective and the tools we need so that we will not be ruled by our human suffering. Instead of becoming unmoored by comparison or personal struggle, we will be reminded that God alone is what truly matters, that nothing should disturb or frighten us, for as St. Teresa of Avila noted, "Whoever has God lacks nothing; God alone suffices."

We can't escape these human emotions because God doesn't want us to. He is not a *mean* God who is jealous of our attention. He is an *awesome* God who is, yes, jealous of our attention. But I know now, because I have tasted it in some small fashion, that God wants to offer us the living water because it is so much better for our souls than comparing our lives with the good things other people have. He pursues us so that we can live a life of real freedom and joy. He goes after us because he wants us to enjoy our life and not be weighed down by burdens that are not ours to bear. God wants to get our attention, and he uses our emotions and reactions to our circumstances as a way of helping us get our interior life in order.

One of the biggest healings God has given me has been an ordered sense of the truth of my identity in Jesus. I knew that I was loved by God, and that God made me. I knew I was special to him, but I couldn't shake this feeling that I had to earn God's love. At the end of every day, as I thought over what was good about that day and what I needed to work on, there was this underlying attitude that my efforts to do good, to do better, would move me further up the ladder of God's approval. God wanted me do to what was right, and my job was to grow in virtue so God could draw me closer to him.

But this was a misguided notion. Yes, God wanted me to grow in virtue. Yes, God wanted to draw me closer to him. But this was not a "contingent" relationship—God didn't draw me closer to him as a reward for my virtuous efforts. It was a friendship relationship, based in truth. The more I understood who God made me to be, to the core of my existence, the freer I became. This was not about my gifts and abilities. This was knowing that who I am is someone known and loved by God, someone who has her Creator deep within her spirit, and connecting with him in a way no other human can. The more the focus shifted from what I can do to who I am, the more I could live as the truest version of myself. I became so aware of God's great love for me, of his great handiwork in who I am, that I no longer look to my external circumstances for my affirmation.

Or not so much, anyway.

Remember, God gave us gifts and abilities, and he wants us to use those for his glory and for our own enjoyment. He loves who he made you to be! But going deeper, drinking the living water instead of water that will never truly satisfy, means that our gifts are not the core of our identity. When I understand and love who God made me to be, that means loving something much deeper than the stuff in life I'm good at. My union with God goes deeper than being thankful for my vocation and station in life.

It goes deeper than embracing the season of suffering—or great satisfaction—that I might currently be in.

What this deep union with God means is that I begin to find my truest sense of who I am in that connection with my Creator.

As Henri Nouwen wrote in *Life of the Beloved*, the more we begin to seek out this voice that calls to us, the more we thirst for it. Not because this voice does not satisfy, but because it satisfies so deeply that our soul is healed in this sacred space: "When our deepest truth is that we are the Beloved and when our greatest joy and peace come from fully claiming that truth, it follows that this has to become visible and tangible in the ways we eat and drink, talk and love, play and work."[2]

You are God's chosen one. This is your truth. It's a truth that your soul knows in its core, and the restlessness you experience is your soul seeking out the proof of this truth. We were made for more than the world tells us is available. We were made for more than the world tells us is possible. Our deep fulfillment can come to us now, in whatever season we might be in.

Jesus sits at the well, waiting to meet us in the midst of our daily chores and cares. He's wants to offer the water that will deeply quench what your soul desires—the truth of its beloved-ness, its chosenness, its worth.

Once we begin to experience this truth, our soul will only be satisfied with this living water. Nothing but the peace of God and this truth of our existence will satisfy. God is pursuing us because he doesn't want us to settle for anything less than what will make us truly happy. The restless feelings within are a sign not of life passing us by but of a deeper thirst that only God can quench.

St. Augustine wrote, "You called and shouted and burst my deafness. You flashed, shone, and scattered my blindness. You breathed odors, and I drew in breath and panted for You. I tasted, and I hunger and thirst. You touched me, and I burned for Your peace."[3]

Turning that restlessness toward God means allowing our soul to be soothed by what it truly seeks. Yes, God gives us gifts and abilities, and we should use them. But we should also put these desires and ambitions in the proper place in our life, and not use them to try to heal and fulfill something that only God can heal.

Nouwen wrote, "Aren't you, like me, hoping that some person, thing, or event will come along and give you that final feeling of inner well-being you desire? Don't you often hope: 'May this book, idea, course, trip, job, country, or relationship fulfill my deepest desire?'"[4]

We can make ourselves crazy trying to solve our inner turmoil with the next external. Planning trips and having adventures and trying new things are all good, but only if we see them for what they are. They are not the solution to the deep longing each of us has within.

God is pursuing us with his transformative love, with the water that will satisfy the very depths of our soul. Our wounds are healed by this truth. Our spirit is settled. The lies we have come to believe—small and big—are redeemed by God's deep, abiding love.

EIGHT

FULFILLMENT

Faith brings into our lives such freedom, such love, such peace, and such joy that there are no words in any language that can explain it. You have to have it in order to know it. You have to experience it in order to understand it. Faith liberates. It liberates love and hope. If I am free to love and free to hope, what more do I want of life?

—Catherine Doherty

The woman at the well admits to Jesus she is not married. She allows him to be a part of her sin and suffering. She trusts him with her past and her present. She is changed. The woman is so transformed that she goes back to the town to bring others to the well. The living water has filled her. She has been restored. She is no longer defined by what she does or even what she has done. She is so much more than that.

The bio in my high school senior yearbook says I planned to be a nurse. I remember wanting to be a nurse, dental hygienist, or physician's assistant. This was alongside my deep desire to be a nun, or at least be chosen by God to do something radical with my life. Basically, my plan was be a nun or complete one of these two-year medical degrees. I would major in biology for two years at the local university in my hometown of Augusta and then head over to the medical school to finish.

During my freshman year of college, I lived in a household of single women discerning their vocation (or waiting on it) who prayed together daily and supported each other spiritually. Three of my roommates were fellow college students, one was an architect shifting gears, the head was a full-time teacher in her mid-forties, and then there was Katharina, a woman several years younger than the teacher who happened to be a physician's assistant.

Katharina drove a very sweet, bright red Honda Prelude. Her room was decorated from her travels to exotic places such as New Zealand and the Caribbean, and she was an excellent baker who helped me gain the freshman fifteen while keeping herself perfectly skinny.

One night at dinner, Katharina was describing her day to the rest of us. She worked at the town's veterans' hospital, where most of her patients were men who had fought in war. The part of her story that stuck out to me involved her walking into a room with a stranger and looking at his body parts. Because that's what a medical caregiver does.

I had not thought through that aspect of the career, having mostly focused on the logistics of how long a program would take and where I would go to school to get the degree. I had totally failed to consider what each of my target professions would actually entail—tasks like drawing blood, scraping teeth, or looking at body parts.

There at the dinner table on that weekday night, my dreams of being a physician's assistant died. That the profession wasn't for me was as clear as the fluid in a bag of . . . fluids.

But God is kind, and he really does have a plan.

A few weeks before this, I had started a new term of college with a new set of classes. My English professor was incredibly encouraging, and I was doing really well in her class. She liked my writing style and encouraged me a lot. This made me think about my high school English teacher, Mr. D., who always felt like my own personal cheerleader. (Just in writing. Mr. D. was also our varsity basketball coach, and I didn't get quite that level of affirmation on the court.)

Writing. Hmmmm. Maybe this was something I should consider.

I set up an appointment with my professor to ask her what she thought. She gave me great ideas about different careers for writers, and that very day, I walked around campus, got the forms signed and submitted, and changed my major. I was now pursuing a communications degree.

Not long after that, I connected a bunch of dots and realized this had always been my gift. I love news and had grown up reading the newspaper and forcing my family to watch me deliver fake episodes of the evening news. I started researching journalism programs and decided I would transfer to the bigger university in Athens, Georgia, after two years so that I could get a journalism degree and become a newspaper reporter.

It was a perfect fit. All those years of my mom having to remind me that "curiosity is not a *need* to know" really jived with being a reporter. In this field, I would get paid for asking a bunch of questions and telling other people what I found out! This was living my dream.

While working on my journalism degree, I arranged a three-month internship at the paper back in Augusta. I took a few classes in Augusta as a transient student while completing the internship and also lined up a job at the paper for after graduation. Two months after graduation, while working at the paper as a clerk, writing stories and obituaries, Paul and I married. I learned so much at that job, but there was a problem: it was second-shift. Paul was working as an attorney keeping normal-people hours, while I would leave for work at three o'clock in the afternoon and get home around midnight. We were newlyweds who never saw each other. It seemed like a bad plan.

After a year of this, I applied for graduate school a hundred miles away in Athens. I made every deadline at the last minute—took and passed the GRE the day before the numbers were due; sent in my application in the day before it was due; and was accepted about three weeks before classes started.

The whole time this was going on, I was asking God to close the door if it wasn't meant to be. It seemed pretty crazy to apply for an out-of-town graduate program since we were settled in Augusta. We had bought a house a few months before we got married, and Paul had decided to hang a shingle and go out on his own in immigration law. And if not seeing each other because I was working second shift was hard, how hard was pursuing our dreams in different towns going to be?

But I had this dream of getting that master's degree before I had kids. I had this desire, these abilities, and a sense of purpose with it all. I figured we would have two or three children, and getting this goal out of the way just made sense.

Except it also made no sense.

In this crazy season, I really did ask God to close any door that he didn't want me walking through. Though I had Paul's full support, I took it one step at a time. GRE, passed. Application, turned in. Program status, accepted.

But I didn't have housing lined up. We had no extra money and had actually sold one of our cars for the cash. We were flying by the seat of our pants, and here I was, going off for another degree. I wasn't quite sure exactly how the advanced degree would fit into all this, but I trusted God was in the middle of these efforts.

I found a place to live a few miles off campus. Since we were down to one car, Paul would drive me up for the week and pick me up to come home a few days later. I had a bike that I planned to ride to and from campus each day.

Except I took one bike ride through the busy streets of this college town, and that was it. I couldn't do it. Even though I was just a few miles from campus, maneuvering through city traffic and campus buses felt too life-threatening. There was no way I could make this setup work, so I started asking classmates if anyone needed a roommate. But of course, no one did—they had all made arrangements months ago.

I decided to look into living on campus, which would be perfect for someone without a car. Campus Housing told me I could get on a waiting list for the graduate dorms, but the only housing spots still available were in the high-rise dorm nicknamed "The Well." I walked over to The Well to check it out and discovered I would be a twenty-three-year-old married woman living with hundreds of college freshmen. Not ideal, but what choice did I have? I called Paul, and we decided it would really just be about six months, as I could commute from home during my last quarter if I'd had enough.

So I headed back to Campus Housing to secure my spot. I walked into the office just as the man at the front desk was hanging up the phone.

"I'm here to get a room at The Well," I told him, "and also to get on a waiting list."

"Let me guess," he replied, "You want to live in the graduate dorm."

I told him I did, and he smiled. He had just gotten off the phone with a woman canceling her spot there. He let me bypass the list, and put me in the nicer, much calmer graduate dorm. It was the final hurdle in a situation that had made little sense on paper and ended up working out with perfect peace.

By the end of that year, I was pregnant with Ethan and did indeed commute to my classes the last quarter. I worked on my thesis the following year and went back for graduation with my nine-month old baby in my arms. It was glorious.

And then I framed my diplomas and kept having babies.

Life really is a mystery. I felt fulfilled pursuing my gifts as a writer. I felt fulfilled working in the newsroom. I loved being a graduate student and getting that degree. Then I completely switched gears and started staying home with my babies—and strangely, I found that really fulfilling as well. I enjoyed the daily tasks of motherhood. It was new and exciting.

But of course there were moments when I felt like life was passing me by. Some days are just hard. But within me, I felt a sense of extraordinary adventure was out there. I just needed time.

But here is the interesting juxtaposition of life and especially of recognizing God's hand in our lives: God gives us interests and gifts and abilities. He gives us a vocation. He has a special call for each one of us, a way that we operate and do business and interact with the world around us.

All of these things come together as we move forward in life, and God wants to meet us in the middle of all of that. Jesus waits for the woman at the well, where she is doing her daily work. He doesn't create a magical space and time to reveal himself to her. He knows what she has going on in her life and waits to meet her in the midst of it.

As each of us moves through our day, Jesus is waiting. The practical aspects of our ordinary lives can cause us great joy and also great fatigue. And Jesus wants to be a part of it.

The slight shift in this narrative is that Jesus wants to be a part of it—but he also wants us to find fulfillment from more than just what we do. He wants to help us dream bigger and have a bigger sense of purpose in our lives. He wants to take what is ordinary and make it extraordinary, not by transforming what we do but transforming how we see ourselves and our lives. He wants to be there to quench our thirst when the ins and outs of our daily lives become a grind, which they certainly can do.

Too often we take this pinched feeling to mean something is really wrong.

I'm bored at my job, we think. I must need to shift gears.

My marriage feels stale; it must be time for something new.

I'm tired of being at home; I need a new adventure.

There's a fine line, isn't there, between seeking a change of scenery and suddenly upending your entire life because you don't like how things feel inside your heart.

We have dreams and goals, aspirations, and a sense of life being more than just the simple thing in front of us. And that's okay. God doesn't want us to settle for mediocrity. He wants us to dream big and go after things. That drive and ambition is not bad.

But God is a god for all seasons. This means you don't need to feel like your happiness is on hold until the big, grand adventure comes along. It also means that you don't need to abandon your responsibilities to go after happiness. This is the great lie we are being sold—that if our life feels unfulfilling right now, it must be time to chase something better.

Not true! That feeling of deep unhappiness is really your soul searching for its Creator. It is your built-in programming redirecting you to what will actually make you happy.

Jesus sits and waits for you, right now. He knows the duties of your day, and he wants to meet you there. He wants you to find great satisfaction in knowing that the thing you are doing right now is the thing he is asking you to do. He doesn't expect you to settle for a lifetime of chores that you hate; he asks you to trust him in this moment.

Do you believe God gave you hopes and dreams and abilities?

Do you believe God has a plan for you?

Do you trust in God's timing in your life?

Do you believe that God can dream bigger than you can?

Do you trust that God's ways are not always our ways but that what he has to offer you will bring satisfaction deeper than anything your human mind might settle for?

So often in life we have to walk in faith. We can only use our human brain—the brain God gave us—because that's how we make decisions. We consider the facts, assess the situation, and throw in some common sense as we move through life. And then God offers to blow our minds with his ways. He tells us he has water that will fulfill us in ways we didn't know were possible. Can we afford to take him up on this offer? Can we afford not to?

What do you want from your life?

Staring out into the grand adventure of life at the starting line of college, I wanted to be really awesome at everything I did. I wanted to make changes and help others, to make a difference and find satisfaction in my efforts. I wanted to love and be loved and to create a home with cute children who brought me joy. Did I understand everything else that life brings?

God walked beside me as I pursued my own personal dreams and gently guided me with grace and peace when things shifted.

When I suffered a miscarriage just before our first anniversary, God used that suffering to draw Paul and me closer to each other.

When God sent us a bunch of baby boys, he used that openness to life to help me die to some of my own selfishness. He used our six children to help me realize how love expands in ways you never knew were possible.

When I pursued too many volunteer activities at once, God allowed that burnout to push me to start to seek his voice for peace in my life. He used that reset as a time for me to begin to see that my worth does not derive from what I do. God began to reveal to me that he was there, sitting at the well, as I scurried about in my daily duties. And what he had to offer me would change my world, opening my eyes to the wonders of his love— his love for my husband, my children, and especially for me.

Because the more I accept God's love and seek union with him, the more love I have to give those around me. The more I am filled by God's love, the more fulfilled I feel. I begin to see my worth as coming not from the many grand adventures God will surely provide but from his goodness. This is a truth that does not change according to the season and time. It is constant, unwavering.

It is all we need.

It isn't bad to have hopes and dreams. But we need to know that our deepest hopes and dreams will be fulfilled only in our union with Jesus. The things we do aren't the key to freedom, fulfillment, or joy—and they aren't a barrier to them either. The more we accept what Jesus offers—the living water, the water that will truly satisfy—the more fulfilled we will be.

NINE

MISSION

The woman left her water jar and went into the town and said to the people, "Come see a man who told me everything I have done. Could he possibly be the Messiah?" They went out of the town and came to him.

—John 4:28–29

What is the point of having it all figured out anyway? Each of us wants to do something grand with our lives; that's the beautiful, positive motivating force behind a desire to be fulfilled. I see the flow of this as something like this:

1. God made me.
2. He gave me abilities and skills.
3. I seek to figure out what I want to do with my life, what I was made for, what will bring me great personal joy.
4. I settle on a career, hopefully something that makes me feel good.
5. About that same time, I begin to pray about my vocation. Maybe that happens just before, maybe at the same time. Maybe I get the vocation aspect of life figured out after I have started my "grown-up job."
6. I work and move forward in life. I seek fulfillment.
7. My job brings me joy. I begin to realize that people are more important.

8. Perhaps my job lends itself to my feeling like I'm making a difference. Maybe being a mom or dad or really excellent aunt or uncle fills that void.
9. Still, I was made for more.
10. But I've got a job I love. I've got a family I love. (*Or* I've got a job that's okay. I love my family, but adulting is really hard.)
11. I was made for more than this. No offense, but this can't be all there is.

Number 11 is the kicker—you *were* made for more! Even with all the really excellent things in your life, even when you get through the in-between, challenging season of thinking maybe life is passing you by, you will come to a place where the things of this world truly will not bring the deep satisfaction you crave or fulfillment of that longing you have deep inside you.

Some people will go through their entire lifetime not understanding this feeling. These days, you get can pretty far in life managing to ignore your feelings. We never have to be alone anymore, never have to sit in silence if we don't want to. We check our email at the stop light. We text someone while waiting at the checkout line. We watch random videos while falling asleep. Our brains are on constant overload, and we stay so stimulated and busy that we can tune out the feeling that something is missing.

But in the silence, whenever you find it, your heart is searching.

And if you allow it to connect with its Creator, you will begin to hear the answers you are seeking.

You are made for more.

You are created for something grand.

You are God's beloved.

Life is wonderful.

The woman at the well heard Jesus's offer, considered it, and took a step in faith. She trusted the Lord, that what he promised was true. Jesus saw her suffering, her wounds from a sinful past—and he also saw who she truly was. She was not her past, not her sins. She was his beloved, and she deserved all the riches of God's kingdom.

The woman at the well accepted this offer, and she was changed. She was so convinced by the truth of the living water that after she received God's grace and love in that moment, she ran back to her town to tell everyone about it.

She wanted others to have this same chance for change. Once you have been touched in your most wounded, raw, hurting places—once you know the freedom that comes from Jesus shining his light on those areas and taking the burdens you thought you would always have to carry, you can't help but share this freedom with others.

You want others to experience this great love because it is so good. And the more you begin to accept the deep love of Jesus, the more you are overcome with love for others.

Going out and preaching the Gospel sounds lofty, like really grand, mission-level preaching. And that is some people's experience. They encounter Jesus, Jesus works a miracle in their life, and after that, all they want to do is share about Jesus. They don't want to keep this secret to themselves.

For many people, their mission field is loving those whom God has placed in their path, not necessarily traveling halfway around the world to love others. But the reality of living as one of Jesus's disciples is that we must learn to love the people we encounter, which means these are very likely people from our day-to-day life. That can be a little less romantic. Loving strangers is oftentimes much easier for me. I don't know much about them, and I've only got to be nice to them for about five to ten minutes. Somehow it's much less work to love the poor and help the needy than to be kind to the family member currently getting on my last nerve.

Catherine Doherty wrote something called "The Little Mandate," which she believed came to her from Jesus. This rule of life guided her.

> Arise—go! Sell all you possess. Give it directly, personally to the poor. Take up My cross (their cross) and follow Me, going to the poor, being poor, being one with them, one with Me.
>
> Little—be always little! Be simple, poor, childlike.
>
> Preach the Gospel with your life—without compromise!
>
> Listen to the Spirit. He will lead you.
>
> Do little things exceedingly well for love of Me.
>
> Love . . . love . . . love, never counting the cost.
>
> Go into the marketplace and stay with Me.
>
> Pray, fast. Pray always, fast.
>
> Be hidden. Be a light to your neighbour's feet. Go without fears into the depths of men's hearts. I shall be with you.
>
> Pray always. I will be your rest.[1]

Here is a woman who was all in for Jesus, and the heart of her mission was little things, not big, grand statements.

In college, I was a youth minister for a few years. On one of our retreats, I received a vision for myself—a sense of who I thought God wanted me to be. That I remember this image from almost thirty years ago speaks to its importance in my life. Every few years God reminds me of what he showed me.

The vision I received as we prayed was an image of myself standing somewhere on the steps of a giant, marble-clad government building, wearing a gorgeous pink suit and really great high heels. I was taking a stand for life. I was speaking to a large group of onlookers, and the words I spoke were truth.

That was the extent of it, but this vision has stayed with me. I think God has used it as a weathervane, a reminder to me of the purpose he set before me at the front end of my adult life. There I was, a college student, trying to figure out what really mattered. What would I do with this *one* life I got from God? I sure didn't want to waste it.

I wanted to feel fulfilled, to use my gifts. I wanted to be a part of the solution, not a part of the problem. I wanted to build God's kingdom, and in my mind's eye as a college student, this involved wearing an excellent suit and excellent shoes. And using my voice. And taking a stand.

Here I am, all these years later. That vision is still with me, and I think I'm starting to understand what it means. I'm not convinced I will ever run for office or even wear that fabulous outfit. I don't know that my speaking opportunities or writing achievements will necessarily bring me to the marble steps of a government building. But taking a stand for life—that's the heart of being fueled by God's love and sharing it with others.

In that moment, I believe, God allowed me to see myself as he sees me—as someone who can be heard in the arena into which he sends me: capable of spreading a message, of saying it in a way that could be received, and armed with the proper information and credentials and a willingness to go where Jesus would send me.

In some ways, this vision of being heard has come true, but it's not in grand arenas. It's in loving the cashier at the grocery store. It's in being willing to tell someone they are deeply loved by God if I feel that God wants me to say it. It's in pushing against my desire to tune out my family when they need me to listen. It's in being patient with my next-door neighbors (who happen to be my parents in one direction and my father-in-law in another) and having boundaries but also a willingness to love them.

I'm armed with the tools I need to take a stand for life—every life. And so are you.

You are capable and articulate and armed with credentials. God has given you a special gift—a desire to be loved by him and to hear his voice—and he wants you to share that with everyone in your path.

What this looks like will be different for each of us. That's a relief. It's personalized. How does God want *you* to share his love? Ask him that, and then do it. Your call to evangelize will be unique to your personal gifts and your personality. Also, it will dovetail perfectly with where you are at in life.

The woman at the well was touched and transformed, and she wanted everyone to know about this living God and his living water. She ran back to town and obviously, based on John's account, got people's attention. Whatever she said was compelling because the people of the town followed her back to the well and got on board with the message of the living God and his living water.

She believed. She was transformed. She evangelized. It changed lives.

And evangelization for her involved a walk back to her neighbors. She didn't climb on a boat and travel halfway around the world. She walked home, and she told the people she already knew. She told them what Jesus had done for her, and they were changed.

What has Jesus done for you? What are you willing to let him do? Let him into all these areas. Ask him what he wants for your life. If you start there, you can never go wrong.

Ask him, and do not be afraid.

I'm amazed at how many times I think I know what Jesus will tell me and he just blows my mind with a totally different answer. I think Jesus will speak words that make me feel trapped in a life I don't want—and he speaks words of adventure. I think he will speak words of condemnation—and he speaks words of freedom. I think I will have to suffer—and he tells me I will never be alone.

I want to do what God's will is for me. And little by little I'm learning to allow this to all be in God's time. Even when I'm tempted to carve out my dreams in my own time frame, I know that won't be best. I don't want these things in my own time. I want them in God's time for my life because God knows better than I know.

We want something grand for our lives. But a willingness to go really deep with Jesus will change you in ways you never knew you could change. God has healed me of so much pettiness and anxiety, of fear and doubt. I'm not walking on clouds, mind you, but the person God has allowed me to become, by giving me grace to release my tight grip on my personal plans and offering them over to him, is far beyond who I could have dreamed myself to be. And it's the best way to live.

The reality of life is that most of the time we will be just living it. You might have lofty dreams and goals—that's awesome. Go for them! I will always support people in their dreams unless those dreams are completely counter to their vocation. But as someone who, in a postpartum haze, once plotted to escape my own house and run away from my family, I'm a big believer in always having someone around to speak a little common sense.

Go after those dreams! You've got this! But also be willing to recognize that those dreams of yours won't solve all your problems. Your personal goals and to-do list won't fill the God-sized hole in your heart. That hole is there because God doesn't want you to be satisfied with the veneer of this world. The world is beautiful and filled with wonder, but it is fleeting and nothing compared to the riches of heaven.

And the minute you stop making your life all about you, you will be amazed at how happy you start to become. "You will have found Christ," wrote Flannery O'Connor, "when you are concerned with other people's sufferings and not your own."[2] In a world that tells us our own pursuits should be the center of our universe, stop to consider that perhaps that isn't true.

What is God asking of me?

Why am I afraid to wait for that answer?

Do I trust Jesus enough to give him everything—my hopes, dreams, time, energy, and abilities? Do I trust that Jesus will take care of me?

For my fortieth birthday, Paul took me to Italy. We visited Rome, Assisi, and Pisa, and also Vicopisano, the small castle town where the Family Balducci comes from. It was glorious.

We arrived in Rome on my birthday, and our friend Fr. Tim had a car waiting at the airport to take us to an apartment on the campus of the Pontifical North American College, where he was a spiritual director. We quickly changed before heading over to meet the Holy Father at his weekly general audience in St. Peter's Square. I was equal parts in awe of this moment and trying very hard to stay awake. (Fr. Tim said we weren't allowed to nap because it would take days to get us back on schedule. We had to soldier through.)

Three days after our arrival in Rome, Fr. Tim, Paul, and I had just finished a late-evening dinner in a tiny restaurant just off St. Peter's Square when my phone rang, which was weird because it hadn't worked at all since we arrived in Rome. It was a Georgia number, so I knew I needed to answer it.

It was Fr. Tim's sister Susie, one of my dearest friends, and she was in a panic. They were at the emergency room with her dad, who had coded. I immediately handed the phone to Fr. Tim, who calmly received the news from his sister. He hung up, we got the check, and the three of us headed over to St. Peter's Square.

For the next thirty minutes, we walked the square and prayed the Rosary. It's a blessing to be with Fr. Tim and Paul in such a scary time because they both have the peace that passes understanding. Paul's mom died unexpectedly when she was forty-nine, so he had endured and survived this kind of suffering and knew God was bigger and would see us through.

Just as we finished the Rosary, my phone rang again. It was Susie's husband, Dennis, calling to deliver the devastating news that Fr. Tim's dad had died.

Though I wanted to cancel the rest of our trip, to fly home and be with Susie, Fr. Tim, their sisters, and their mom, they assured us we needed to keep traveling. And so we said goodbye to Fr. Tim the next morning at the train station as he headed back to the United States, and we traveled on to Assisi.

My takeaway from that experience, sad as it was, was a powerful reminder that God will take care of you. Perhaps you are afraid to say yes to Jesus because you don't know what it will cost, but I promise you that you will always stay on his radar. I'm not saying you will never suffer. I'm saying he will protect you and guide you and keep you in his care.

When Fr. Tim said yes to going back to Rome, he did not imagine his dad would die while he was out of the country. And yet God sent one of his very dearest friends to be with him and pray with him in that moment of grief. Fr. Tim was off saying yes to Jesus and evangelizing to the far ends of the earth, but we were there with him in St. Peter's Square when he most needed support. Jesus made sure Tim was cared for. Fr. Tim would have been okay on his own, and Jesus went the extra mile for him anyway.

If you want to change the world, love your family. Love the people God puts in your path. Know that you are loved by your Creator, and you will have everything you need to love those around you.

It will blow your mind the things God will do. He will give you the words you need to say, the wisdom to say yes when you should and no when you need to. He will pour out a special love for whomever he puts in your path. It will feel miraculous; it will feel like a grand adventure to live with this kind of freedom and love.

Trust in the Lord. You will be fulfilled.

ADDITIONAL RESOURCES

Catherine Doherty, *Poustinia: Christian Spirituality of the East for Western Men*

Joyce Meyer, *Battlefield of the Mind*

Fr. Henri Nouwen, *Life of the Beloved*

Fr. Jacques Philippe, *Searching for and Maintaining Peace, The Way of Trust and Love*

Fr. Mike Schmitz, "What Does Surrender Actually Look Like?" https://www.youtube.com/watch?v=aabwei87sQM

Fr. Emmerich Vogt, *Detaching with Love* audio series

The Cloud of Unknowing

NOTES

1. ENCOUNTER

1. John Paul II, Address at 15th World Youth Day Vigil of Prayer, August 19, 2000, 5, https://www.vatican.va/content/john-paul-ii/en/speeches/2000/jul-sep/documents/hf_jp-ii_spe_20000819_gmg-veglia.html.

2. Catherine Doherty, "Duty of the Moment," chap. 12 in *Dear Parents: A Gift of Love for Families* (Combermere, Ontario: Madonna House Publications, 1997).

2. THIRST

1. Augustine, *Tractates on the Gospel of John*, 15:11.

4. TRUST

1. Augustine, *Confessions*, bk. 1, chap. 1, par. 1.

5. CONVERSION

1. Catherine Doherty, *Poustinia: Christian Spirituality of the East for Western Men* (Notre Dame, IN: Ave Maria Press, 1975), 72.

2. Jacques Philippe, *The Way of Trust and Love: A Retreat Guided by St. Thérèse of Lisieux* (New York: Scepter, 2012), 94.

3. Philippe, *Way of Trust and Love*, 94.

6. SURRENDER

1. John Paul II, Address at 15th World Youth Day, 5.

2. John Paul II, Address at 15th World Youth Day, 5.

7. HEALING THROUGH TRUTH

1. Henri Nouwen, *Life of the Beloved: Spiritual Living in a Secular World* (New York: Crossroad, 2002), 33.

2. Nouwen, *Life of the Beloved*, 47.

3. Augustine, *Confessions*, bk. 10, chap. 27.

4. Nouwen, *Life of the Beloved*, 34–36.

9. MISSION

1. Catherine Doherty, "The Little Mandate," https://www.madonnahouse.org/mandate/.

2. Flannery O'Connor to "A.," *The Habit of Being*, ed. Sally Fitzgerald (New York: Farrar Straus Giroux, 1979).

RACHEL BALDUCCI is a writer, blogger, speaker, and cohost of *The Gist* on Catholic TV. She teaches journalism at Augusta University.

She is the author of *How Do You Tuck in a Superhero?*, *Make My Life Simple*, and *Overcommitted*. She has been a columnist for the *Southern Cross* for fifteen years, served as a reporter for the *Augusta Chronicle*, and taught middle school and high school English and history at Alleluia Community School.

Balducci earned a bachelor's degree from Georgia State University and a master's degree from the University of Georgia. She was a regular guest on the *Jen Fulwiler Show* and has appeared on many Catholic TV and radio shows.

She lives with her husband, Paul, and their six children in Augusta, Georgia.

rachelbalducci.com
Facebook: Rachel Balducci, Testosterhome
Twitter: @rachelbalducci
Instagram: @rachelbalducci
Pinterest: @RachelBalducci
YouTube: Rachel Balducci

AVE

AVE MARIA PRESS

Founded in 1865, Ave Maria Press,
a ministry of the Congregation of
Holy Cross, is a Catholic publishing
company that serves the spiritual and
formative needs of the Church and its
schools, institutions, and ministers;
Christian individuals and families; and
others seeking spiritual nourishment.

For a complete listing of titles from

Ave Maria Press

Sorin Books

Forest of Peace

Christian Classics

visit www.avemariapress.com

AVE MARIA PRESS
Notre Dame, IN
A Ministry of the United States Province of Holy Cross